BEER FESTIVALS

A Great British Tradition

LAURA HADLAND

CAMRA

Dedicated to Mike
who has supported me for 25 years,
but only got to visit one of the
beer festivals mentioned in this book.

Published by the Campaign for Real Ale Ltd
230 Hatfield Road, St Albans, Hertfordshire AL1 4LW
camra.org.uk/books

© Campaign for Real Ale Ltd. 2025

The rights of Laura Hadland to be identified as the
author of this Work have been asserted by her in accordance
with the Copyright, Designs and Patents Act 1988.

First published 2025

ISBN 978-1-85249-395-0

A CIP catalogue record for this book is available from the British Library

Printed and bound in the United Kingdom by Short Run Press, Exeter

Managing Editor: Alan Murphy
Design / Typography: Dale Tomlinson
Sales & Marketing: Madeleine Hardman
Cover illustration: Simon Gane

....

The images in this book were supplied by Laura Hadland,
except where indicated otherwise.

....

Contents

Introduction

BEER and cider festivals are rarely described as significant
cultural events, but they undoubtedly are. They have been
mainstays of the British drinking calendar for more than 50
years. What's more, festivals have played a huge role in shaping
the beer landscape of the UK, in all its richness and diversity.

The most successful – and long-lasting – beer festivals
were pioneered by the Campaign For Real Ale (CAMRA).
For that reason, this book is being launched as the consumer
organisation celebrates a half century of national beer
festivals in 2025.

CAMRA arguably created the festival template that is
still followed by scores of events each year. But beer festival
culture has taken on a life of its own, growing and evolving
into new forms. What follows in these pages is an homage to
these events, which showcase and shape the beer and cider
landscape. It is a gesture of appreciation to all of the people
who make them happen.

So, grab a glass, buy some tokens and join me on a
leisurely stroll around British (and Irish) beer festivals past
and present. We'll take in the origins of the beer festival in
these islands. I'll tell you how a beer festival operates, and,
more importantly, who runs it, be they volunteers, producers
or paid staff. It is their stories that bring this book to life.

I don't claim for a moment that this is a comprehensive guide. It isn't a guidebook at all, although I hope it will offer a little travel inspiration. Nor is it intended to highlight 'The Best' to the exclusion of all others. One of the things that makes the thousands of beer festivals across the UK so wonderful is that they are all different. They are shaped by their venue, their organisers, their communities, and more often than not, the brewing scene in their area. Instead, I present you with a compendium of experiences that I hope will whet your appetite sufficiently to encourage you to pull up a chair (if you can find one) and tuck in to the fine institution that is the great British beer festival for yourself.

WHAT IS A BEER FESTIVAL?

I APPROACHED this question with some trepidation. There have been so many beer festivals, and they vary so wildly. How could I pin down a succinct explanation?

Happily, breaking down the name made things clearer. Festival entered our language by way of the Medieval Latin *festivalis* – a religious holiday or feast day. The Merriam-Webster dictionary sets out two definitions for the word festival:

1. A time of celebration marked by special observances

2. An often periodic celebration or program of events or entertainment having a specified focus

Merriam-Webster's second definition directly addresses the matter at hand. An event with a specific focus. For us that is beer, cider and perry. Easy.

What I find much more interesting is the word that links these two definitions: celebration. That is the key. A festival of beer, cider and/or perry is an entertaining affair where the attendees come along primarily because of their shared love of those drinks. The beverages are delighted in and honoured.

There may be music (and love, and, indeed, romance). There could be games. It is not unheard of to find traditional country dancing, dog shows, comedy performances or a small concession selling pork pies.

But the primary focus is the liquid. The celebration of beer. The great wonder of the many varieties of apple used to make cider. The deep mysteries of silken perry.

*   *   *

Since our definition puts the drink at the heart of our festival, we cannot confuse beer festivals with music festivals – although the line between them, and the motivation to attend them, is increasingly blurred.

I was surprised to see a vast array of cask-conditioned ale and real cider on offer at bars dotted around the expansive site of the four-day Shrewsbury Folk Festival. There is a real confluence between the types of people who are inclined towards folk music and a great quality pint, I was told by Nigel Smith. He is the owner of Moongazing Hare Bars, who offer cask ale-focused bar hire for festivals.

As we chatted there, a couple of morris men with painted faces walked up to the bar to order a brace of pints and shoot the breeze with the bartenders. The staff are all experienced professionals. They know what they are selling and how it should taste.

Nigel takes the complexity of ordering and installing a cask ale bar away from music festival organisers, who, in most cases, wouldn't know where to begin.

People are limited in how much money they've got in their pockets. They want to make sure they spend that money on something worthwhile and different. They want something of quality rather than just Eurofizz. The organisers here, and at the other festivals where we operate, recognise that their customers are real ale and cider drinkers who appreciate a decent pint as well as a decent bit of music. We understand what these folk festival goers are looking for and we deliver on that, including making sure we've got a wide range of local products.

NIGEL SMITH, Moongazing Hare Bars

At perhaps the other end of the musical spectrum, the organisers of the Bloodstock Open Air heavy rock and metal festival in Derbyshire have a very similar approach to Nigel. They offer over a hundred quality ales and ciders across the various festival bars each year. It's a key part of the festival's attraction. 'It's very important that not only is the range of beer available, but that it's served correctly. We choose our partners very carefully. We don't go with the obvious brands and we don't bring

The Joy Hotel perform at Fyne Fest 2024

in a 'festival lager'. We want to make sure what we're offering is what the fans want, something that's unique and a little bit different. For Bloodstock, that's what works.' (Adam Gregory, Co-Director of Bloodstock Festival.)

So close is the synergy that in 2023 Yorkshire brewer Timothy Taylor's embarked on a major collaboration with the festival. Their new pale ale brand, Hopical Storm, sponsored the New Blood stage – a partnership that continued in 2024. New Blood gives the winners of Metal 2 The Masses, a nationwide talent search, the opportunity to perform in front of the festival crowd.

These examples show us that while the definition of a beer festival may be quite clear, the relationship between music festivals and beer is changing. Organisers are recognising that their fans have a taste for great music as well as quality ale, and they are striving to meet that demand. Culturally, the role of beer in the broader festival category is evolving, but in the interests of keeping a relatively tight focus, we will stick to the true beer festivals, whose history stretches back a surprisingly long way.

Beer Festival History

Early Pioneers

A number of beer and brewing exhibitions took place in the UK and internationally during the 19th and early 20th centuries, like the annual International Exhibition of Hops and Beer and the Brewers' Exhibition. These were trade shows primarily, perhaps after the fashion of SIBA's Beer X these days. One headline in particular caught my eye.

BREWERS 'GO SOFT'
Big Display of Lemonade at Beer Exhibition

The Brewers' Exhibition, which opened at the Agricultural Hall, Islington, London, today, seems at first glance to be devoted to a display of iced lemonade, still lemonade, aerated lemonade, sweet lemonade, dry lemonade and potato crisps.

The real beer show is in an inner hall – almost as big as the main hall. Here casks of beer touch the ceiling in symmetrical piles.

"It is the biggest beer show on earth," said an official. "I know that the main hall, with its tonic water and bottle-washing machines is a bit of a shock to the visitor who comes here expecting to see nothing but beer but actually we have more than enough beer here to supply Wembley on Cup Final day."

Leicester Daily Mercury, Saturday, 31 October 1931

Perhaps the earliest UK beer festival was put on by W. Holland (the people's caterer, apparently) whose Great Show of English and Continental Beer was held at the North Woolwich Gardens (now known as the Royal Victoria Gardens) for five days in May 1873. It was arranged 'for the purpose of comparing and testing the relative values of the productions of the Brewers of Great Britain and the Continent'. The beers were 'arranged in a Pavilion especially erected for that purpose and will be divided into compartments, taking each County in Great Britain', the *Daily News* reported.

The Hour recorded that there were 180 beers from 40 brewers available. This is a truly incredible number of beers. The scale would not be matched again for well over a century. According to historian Ron Pattinson's research, only two of those brewers still exist – the then 18-year-old Donnington Brewery from Stow-on-the-Wold, and Dreher, now Schwechat, of Vienna, who were founded in 1632. Interestingly, Anton Dreher Jr was the first brewer to introduce artificial cellar cooling, which was installed in his Triest (now Trieste) brewery in 1877.

Entertainment came from a variety of musical concerts, and the Dramatic and Farce Company performed 'The Middy Ashore'. Entrance was 6d beyond the usual admission to the gardens, and visitors paid 1s for their 'tasting order' which allowed them to taste the beers. Prices were 'affixed to each Cask' and visitors were asked to vote for their favourite in taste and price.

It was clearly some time in the making. Advertisements in the regional press exhorted brewers to get in touch with the organisers in February 1873 to express their interest in exhibiting. For something over 150 years in the past, it all sounds surprisingly familiar.

John W. Green's Phoenix Brewery of Luton celebrated winning a prize medal for their pale ale 'which cannot be surpassed for its cheapness and exhilarating properties' at the show. The Irish brewers

Messrs Wm. Henry and Co of Newry were said to have received first prize for their porter and stout.

The aptly named Mr Councillor Beer received a gold medal for his pale and strong ales. 'Perhaps some day Canterbury ale will obtain as good a name and as worldwide a fame as the celebrated Burton ales,' hoped *The Canterbury Journal*.

Capers on the Continent

Of course, beer festivals aren't unique to the UK, although they are quite different in character elsewhere, hence why they aren't treated in detail within these pages. Even the mighty Munich Oktoberfest will only receive a passing mention.

Vive la difference! In October 1886 a bread, herring and beer festival was held in the Dutch town of Leyden to celebrate the anniversary of the raising of the siege of that town. Reported in the *Liverpool Echo*, it was marked by the distribution of not just bread, herrings and beer but also cigars to the people alongside processions of trades and concerts. Not all European beer festivals, though, were a moment of celebration, some were set up in the great spirit of competition.

A French beer show has been opened at the Pavillon de La Ville de Paris by M. Barbe, Minister of Agriculture, accompanied by his old professor, M. Chevreul, to whom a bière d'honneur was given to drink to the health and longevity of all his great-grandchildren. The main object of the exhibition is to test the superiority of French beer over German, which is pronounced to be so drugged as to be almost poisonous.

M. Velten, the proprietor of the Brasserie de la Mediterranée, asked the Minister that the duty on French beer should be lessened. After this a run was made for the lunch room to taste the beer. A correspondent who tasted some of the specimens says that though excellent from what in England would be called a thin table beer point of view, they are far behind the ordinary beers of Germany.

East Anglian Daily Times, Saturday, 17 September 1887

A good effort from the French, but more work needed.

The Kilkenny Beer Festival

One of the earliest long-running modern beer festivals took place in Kilkenny, Ireland. The first was organised by Alderman Michael J. McGuinness and Bill Finnegan, the sales manager of the local Smithwicks brewery. The festival ran annually from 1964 at a cost of £30,000. The first iteration ran for seven days and saw 200,000 people come to the Marble City, with families welcome. The carnival-style event was a city-wide affair, including a cavernous beer tent set centre stage, which could accommodate up to 3,000 drinkers at a time, if you were happy to stand.

Revellers enjoying the Kilkenny Beer Festival (courtesy of *The Kilkenny Observer*)

In a multi-faceted programme, which changed from year to year, the festival boasted the inclusion of the Kilkenny Cat Competition (an international event paralleling Crufts), a German marching band, pipe and cigar smoking contests, a doll show and even a tiddlywinks-related World Record attempt. The German bands were authentic, flown over from Bavaria by the festival committee. There was apparently no restriction on what could be included in the festival programme, provided that the majority of the committee liked the idea.

Smithwicks provided a lighter beer made especially for the occasion, and the whole event was based on the Oktoberfest model – right down to waitresses in German costume handing out frothy tankards along the beer festival tables.

Writing in *The Kilkenny Observer*, John Fitzgerald retold a cracking anecdote about one unfortunate farmer who attended that first Kilkenny Festival:

> ...who accidentally spat out his false teeth when he was dancing around the beer tent. He spent the best part of an hour searching under the table amid thousands of pounding feet that were keeping time to the music. Friends tried to console him under the table as he conducted an inch-by-inch search of the frothy, beer-saturated floor.
>
> Prayers were offered to St Anthony by religious folk who knelt beside the table and tried to make themselves heard above the ear-splitting chorus of "For Ever and Ever". When he found his dentures, the farmer thanked the prayer group and the Macra lads who had come to his aid and rejoined the festivities.
>
> He could not have been more joyful or relieved if he had located the mystical Holy Grail or won the Irish Sweep Stake, such was the importance to him of his set of false teeth.

Perhaps one of the strangest anecdotes was the festival's role in the removal of one Father Mulligan from his position as a spiritual director within The Pioneer Association. He had reportedly begun to question whether the Association was too strict in its definition of temperance. In 1969 Mulligan was asked to step down, reports Diarmuid Ferriter in Christian journal *The Furrow,* partly for suggesting 'it would be enlightened to introduce children to small amounts of alcohol to enable them to grow up with a responsible attitude towards it, and partly because of his extension of best wishes to the organisers of the Kilkenny Beer Festival in the same year.'

The festival is remembered fondly by local residents. The Kilkenny Motor Club waxed lyrical about its heritage when attempting to revive a contemporary version of the festival in 2010: 'This festival was about Irish culture, how alcohol has had a role in almost every aspect of our lives. From weddings to wakes and All-Ireland's to

Grand Slams, alcohol has always been used by Irish people as a way to celebrate life.'

Each year the festival had a huge economic impact on Kilkenny. In his 2009 PhD from NUI Maynooth, James Monagle said that, 'socially and culturally it was to be the catalyst of Kilkenny's rebirth, its re-imaging and its re-growth'.

However, the good-natured joviality that had characterised the earliest years of the Kilkenny Beer Festival were later marred as interlopers from outside – hearing tales of the legendary party – gatecrashed the celebration. An 'invasion of lager louts' from Dublin and elsewhere brought chaos to the event, with one local newspaper headline in 1970 reporting 'Sex Scenes Shock City and Charges of Gross Immorality.' That said, the official Gardai report from the same year in the local press suggested there were 'no serious problems', so the invasion may have been somewhat exaggerated.

Described by one commentator in the *Irish Times* as having 'somewhat questionable cultural credentials', the festival's days were numbered. It was gradually scaled down and tamed, before finally being replaced with the Kilkenny Arts Week, now the Kilkenny Arts Festival, from 1974. Artist, illustrator and Arts Week founder Susan Butler perhaps summarised the reasons for the change of approach the best:

> The Beer festival was enjoyed by very many and much hard work and admirable organisation went into it. Perhaps the dregs of drunken youth, picked from sodden piles in the High St and wafted on trucks by the Gardai, to recover in the fresh air on the gorse prickly slopes of Ossory hill, caused the more thoughtful of the citizens to pause and think; was art, rather than booze, just probably the answer for a city celebration? (Susan Butler, writing in the Kilkenny Arts Week programme, 1995.)

Britain's Beer Festival

One of the earliest English events to self define as a beer festival was Britain's Beer Festival. It was held at Alexandra Palace on the 21st and 23rd–28th October 1972. A lovely black-and-white Movietone newsreel captured the action. We see a Watney's sign on one wall and what looks suspiciously like the infamous Red Barrel font in action pouring frothy halves. Cut to a young lady dispensing Ben Truman Export Draught and a close up of a proper Czech pour of Tuborg being handed out to a guest.

The narrator tells us that the beer is free, and given the number of bar staff and the speed with which drinks are being handed out, it certainly looks like they were included in the ticket price. The event is lively – we are treated to views of groups of guests smiling, chatting and jostling over their beers.

Britain's Beer Festival features in *The Stage* (October 12, 1972)

CAMRA, barely 18 months old at that point, chose not to attend the event because only pressurised beer was on offer. The more established Society for The Preservation of Beers from the Wood, founded in 1963, were banned from holding a stand, the *Daily Mirror* reported, because five big breweries threatened to withdraw their keg beers from the event if they were present. A society spokesman said, 'I think they were afraid of public reaction to real beer,' and the ban led to over 100 SPBW and CAMRA members picketing the event in protest. 'Not only is the beer on display phoney, but the festival isn't national,' remarked CAMRA Chairman and picket leader Christopher Hutt.

A full Scottish marching band and a troupe of Morris dancers performed amongst the crowds, while musical entertainments were offered from the stage. Hundreds of guests watched on from long tables in the packed Great Hall. Most were seated, but a couple of more vigorous young ladies danced on the tables.

The organisers were a London-based theatre company, Impresario Management. They clearly spared no expense on the promotion of the original festival – they took out a postal campaign to market it, with the event's key details stamped as a postmark cover over the stamps of letters.

The event was not well received by many. Punters complained of queues – an hour to get in, 45 minutes to get a drink, and hours to get food. The organisers blamed the volume of attendees for the issues. Despite this, the next year they took the festival to Blackpool's Norbreck Castle Hotel. This time it was billed as a 40-day extravaganza, offering nightly entertainment for holidaymakers looking for a bit of adults-only time. An article in *The Stage* tells us it was planned to be open for five hours a night with the bill featuring the likes of The New Vaudeville Band, The New Faces, and (gulp) Bernard Manning.

They had hoped for 2,000 guests a night, but the event fell flat and was cancelled after just three nights. 'ANGOVER DAY FOR THE BEER FESTIVAL' screamed the *Daily Mirror* headline after drinkers reported queuing for 45 minutes to get a pint on the opening day. Impresario Management said they were unable to continue due to poor attendance. They had sold just a few dozen tickets on the opening nights of the run. The *Manchester Evening News* reported that there were a number of factors responsible for this: 'The high admission fee charge – £2 a head – the four mile journey from Blackpool town centre, poor organisation by the show management, and the beer only rule which was disliked by many women visitors.' (*Manchester Evening News,* Friday, 20 July 1973.)

This high entry charge does suggest that once you were in, the festival was all inclusive. But given that the average price of a pint was around 15p at the time, £2 does sound like a big ask. Britain's Beer Festival was replaced with a cabaret show organised by the Norbreck Castle Hotel's own management, who felt it would be much more popular with their guests. Despite the problems, the event spawned a series of similar spin-offs by private enterprises around the country, including a seven-day Tyneside Beer Festival, but none of them were able to generate much of a following.

World Beer Show

The World Beer Show – the so-called 'booze up of the century' – arrived at London's Olympia on the 2nd to 10th August 1974. *The New York Times* billed it as a 'carnival of drink', saying, 'It is expected to be the happiest trade show since the invention of trade shows.'

Eric Wainwright, the 'Good Beer Spy', wrote up his review of the goings on for the *Daily Mail.* Eric wrote for the paper from the mid-50s until around 1977, finding a niche in beer writing during the last decade of his career.

> At the biggest pub in the world I supped the beers of a dozen countries, had my photograph taken with a topless model, and kicked a football through a manager's mouth.
>
> The World Beer Show, a mixture of funshows and the serious stuff, opened yesterday at Olympia. Bars cleared for action – from 3pm to 11pm including Sunday – until August 10.
>
> At the International Bar I sank beers from Luxembourg, Norway, Australia, Czechoslovakia, Spain, France and Japan. I drank the ales of Olde England ... real beer straight from the wood. Brakspear, Adnam, Ruddle, King and Barnes, Gale, Theakston, Fuller, Shepherd Neame, Young, Wadworth. Great names. Bravo the lot!

But the most formidable was EKU, brewed in Bavaria and "The Strongest Beer in the World". A man from the Guinness Book of Records sagged next to me at the bar. Definitely the strongest. It will replace Thomas Hardy Ale in our October edition. Advice: don't drink more than four bottles. And at a supermarket price of 55p a bottle, maybe you won't want to.

At this cheery, beery show, I saw Simba, a lady who danced with a python ... she was billed to eat glass but had a sore throat. But I didn't bother to "Guess the Barmaids Weight"...

I invited them to dinner.

Daily Mail, Saturday, 3 August 1974

Behind all of this happy-go-lucky misogyny, there are a couple of really interesting nuggets of information. We can match up Wainwright's description of the event with a full page advertisement taken out in CAMRA's monthly newsletter, *What's Brewing*, in July 1974. This tells us that admission was £2.50 including 50p of beer vouchers.

What's Brewing September 1974

CAMRA members were enticed with an extra 10% off if they visited on Monday to Thursday, and were offered a free pint at the Ales of Olde England stand – billed as 'real ales served from the wood in the traditional way by independent regional brewers'. Just as Wainwright describes.

His list of breweries is slightly at odds with the advertisement. The *Daily Mail* gives Fullers, Shepherd Neame and Youngs in attendance, perhaps last-minute additions to the stand. The advert tells us that Darley and Higsons beers were also available. As to the International Bar, we discover some of the brands on offer – Brahma, Swan, Asahi, Warteck and Bofferding. Other newspaper reports tell us that cider was on offer, but not who the producer was.

EKU's 'strongest beer in the world' caught my attention. The beer in question was probably the 11% ABV Doppelbock EKU 28, first brewed in the 1950s using an enhanced malt concentration and a slow, nine-month cold fermentation. It was erroneously labelled as hailing from Munich in the *What's Brewing* advertisement. EKU is actually brewed more than 150 miles away by the Kulmbacher Brauwerei in Kulmbach, a small town in Bavaria. I know this because, as fate would have it, I lived in Kulmbach for 18 months as a child, while my father worked for the technology conglomerate Siemens. Sadly, I was too young to make the most of this opportunity, although I did get to enjoy my first taste of beer festival tradition while I was out there, despite having near tee-total parents.

Alcoholic strength wasn't the only thing that brought out the Guinness inspector's clipboard at the World Beer Show. If you wanted a world record for beer-mat flipping ability, this was apparently your golden opportunity.

It's fair to say that the World Beer Show had a mixed reception. The choice of more than 100 beers, cider, lagers and ales did not go unnoticed, but it was something else that caught the attention of the press.

There's soccer, sex, music, towers of strength and even Percy Dalton's Famous Peanut Company.
And there's women – hundreds of delightful barmaids to tempt a taste at each stand, chosen from various agencies, modelling and dancing companies.

The girls don't seem to know much about what they are selling but the patrons don't mind.

After passing a sign saying "all counters at your own risk" you come across Tuppy Owen's sex diary '74 stand. Nude pictures were selling like pints at 5p each.

Hammersmith & Shepherds Bush Gazette, Thursday, 8 August

The organisers seemed to think that sex would sell, and who's to say they were wrong? Chris Hampson for the *Sunday Mirror* felt inclined to concentrate his coverage of the event solely on one particular member of the festival staff.

To a man they raised their glasses and toasted brave model Mary Maxted. And even Mary thought she deserved a vote of thanks after appearing topless and wearing only a pair of flimsy briefs at (wait for it) ... the World Beer Show at London's Olympia. There were compensations, mind you. Mary was paid £40 a day and she was given the heady title of Miss World Beer 1974. But oh, the hazards: Mary's duties involved posing topless for photographs with visitors at the show.

And with all the strong beer around, there were bound to be difficult moments. Said Mary, 24: "When I walked through the crowd there were grabbing hands everywhere. I hung on to my security man for dear life and safety's sake." But that was not all. She said: "On one occasion somebody tried to rip off my briefs. I just held on to what was left and fled for dear life."

Mary, of Dorking, Surrey, posed for more than 500 visitors a day at the show, which closed last night. She said: "I'm bruised all over. Honestly, my bottom is sore with pinching. I do a lot of nude modelling and I don't find it obscene or offensive. In fact, I would have been prepared to pose completely nude at the beer show. Then, there was that attempt to snatch off my briefs and I decided: 'Not on your Nellie.'"

So the lads had to make do with their beer.

Sunday Mirror, Sunday, 11 August 1974

Nothing like a few (hundred) instances of sexual assault to make the time just fly by. Mary was clearly a willing participant in the event and a vocal advocate for the sex industry. But her story did not end well.

Known professionally as Mary Millington from 1974 onwards, Mary was a businesswoman, model and pornographic actress. Actually 28 at the time of the Show, not 24 as reported, Mary sank into a spiral of depression and drug addiction after the loss of her terminally ill mother in 1976. She had nursed her mother for a decade, going into pornography to help pay for her care. Mary had wanted to be a fashion model, but at 4 feet 11 inches was not tall enough.

After experiencing increasing stress following frequent police raids on her sex shop in Tooting, she was found dead in August 1979. Mary's final film appearance was in the Sex Pistols film, 'The Great Rock 'n' Roll Swindle', which neither she nor Sid Vicious lived to see released.

Mary's charms did not impress everyone at the Show. The *Wolverhampton Express and Star* concluded that 'no serious, God-fearing, law-abiding drinker in his right mind should ever set foot in the damn place'. And tacky titillation was not the only thing making jaws drop at the festival. The eye-watering pricing also attracted very strong criticism. British Rail withdrew their package tour trips to the show midway through the week on the basis of complaints about pricing from passengers.

Perhaps unsurprisingly, the Campaign for Real Ale also took a dim view of proceedings. The National Executive had already voted against having a recruitment stand because they would have no control over the quality or service of the beer. Michael Hardman, one of the four founders of CAMRA, reported on the show for *What's Brewing* and was scathing in his criticism of both the beer and the entertainment.

The beer wasn't particularly well kept, which wasn't surprising when none of the bar staff on the opening day had the slightest idea of what a spile was.

The nastiest thing about the whole affair, however, was the existence of stands which turned the event into a cross between a trade show and an orgy. There were stalls pushing souvenirs and pub furniture, a variety of electronic or American bar games, and a set of rugby goalposts which you were supposed to climb, regardless of your state of inebriation. There was also a sex shop, promoting strange-shaped candles, a double-feature film show with such delicacies as Snow White and the Seven Perverts, and a booth where you could have your picture taken with a half-naked woman on your knee.

What's Brewing, September 1974

CAMRA would soon host a national beer festival of their own. Events like Britain's Beer Festival arguably provided some influence on how their ideas were shaped, as did smaller events like the Norwich Bystanders Society's small festival featuring 12 beers in October 1972. But the World Beer Show probably only offered a clear indication of what a beer festival should not be. And I am profoundly grateful for that.

The First CAMRA Beer Festivals

While sporadic beer festivals came and went in the mid-20th century, it was the Campaign For Real Ale (CAMRA) who led the way in defining, organising and popularising the British beer festival as we understand it today.

Founded in 1971, CAMRA is an independent consumer organisation that promotes cask-conditioned ale, full juice cider and perry, as well as pubs and clubs. At its height, the Campaign boasted more than 190,000 members, although membership has declined post-pandemic and now stands at just under 150,000.

Over the decades, their approach to campaigning has been multi-faceted. They have lobbied the government, staged protests, created learning resources and a whole lot more. One of the most important campaigning activities has been, almost since the beginning, the beer festival. These events helped to generate funds as well as bringing real ale to a new audience.

'Festivals were a great way of showing what great beer could be as well as recruiting new members,' says John Cryne, a former National Chairman of the Campaign.

The national organisation is administered via a sizeable network of local branches, many of whom now organise their own festivals each year. In the early days, some branches reached out to licensees primarily as a campaigning action in support of real ale.

Chester and Clwyd branch of CAMRA, the Campaign for Real Ale, have announced details of their forthcoming beer exhibition, to be held during the first week in May.

With a larger scale festival due in late Summer CAMRA see the Spring occasion as very much an opportunity to exhibit various real beers to the free trade generally, licensees, club stewards, hoteliers and restaurateurs.

The beers on exhibition have been chosen for several reasons, perhaps not the least being that their permanent availability within the area would greatly widen the choice of beers.

Reports reaching CAMRA reflect the high demand that exists for real beer and CAMRA point out that those establishments which have recently introduced, or reverted to, real beer report that it has been commercially very successful.

Cheshire Observer, Friday, 25 March 1977

The first Leicester beer festival took place in 1976

As well as introducing the trade to the quality and value of real ale, festivals are an important vehicle for educating the public: 'Festivals are important to show how different beers work for different people – people still don't know what all the differences between beers are. Festivals have so many beers that you can always find people something they like. I have been a publican and there isn't enough time or hand-pumps to do this in the pub.' (Denny Cornell-Howarth, festival volunteer.)

All CAMRA festivals are organised and staffed solely by volunteers. Through their dedication over the last 50 years, the beer festival has become embedded within our cultural consciousness. 'CAMRA is one big family ... We all come together, we give up our annual leave and work 20 hour days to put on the biggest beer festival in the world. Then at the end of the week, we all go back to work!' (Nik Antona, former National Chairman.)

But as CAMRA has an ageing membership, there is a question mark about the viability of the model continuing in the future. Data from the Organisation for Economic Cooperation and Development (OECD) shows that workers have less leisure time than in previous decades, perhaps making younger people unwilling to give up precious holidays for voluntary causes. 'The problem is that the volunteers are getting older. And it's getting harder and harder. It's a three-day festival, but there's the set-up beforehand and there's the take-down afterwards, and that's hard work. We're asking older and older people to volunteer – unfortunately we're the only ones that have got time to do it.' (Terry Lock, former CAMRA National Executive member.)

A good festival also relies on its links with the independent brewing trade. From a professional point of view, I would support festivals every time because I think they are a good way of getting publicity for your beers and make sure you have CAMRA on side. CAMRA have been hugely important for Fuller's. I used to go to the Great British Beer Festival because it was part of my job and I noticed a lot of people would come to the Fuller's bar for their first drink of the day and finish at the bar for the last drink of the day. I think people forget the value of familiarity and consistency in the world of beer. They want to start with something they trust because when they go around the festival some of the beers they try

they won't like as much. A lot of the family brewers produce beers
that are easy to drink and that's why people want to go to them.

JOHN KEELING, former Brewing Director for Fuller's

I got a similar response from the team running the Everards bar at the
Leicester beer festival in 2020. I asked why they would bother having
a brewery bar there when the city is saturated with Everards outlets.
They told me they served the first beer of the day to a huge number of
visitors, who wanted something they knew they could rely on before
embarking on their own tasting adventure.

*   *   *

Some of the earliest CAMRA-run festivals include the Hertfordshire
branch's endeavour at St Alban's Market Hall on 30th March 1974,
and the Cardiff branch's exhibition at the Windsor Hotel, Barry Dock
on 18th May of the same year.

However, the very first was an add-on to the third CAMRA
AGM, held at the Tempest Anderson Hall in York on 9th March 1974,
which attracted members from all over the country. An exhibition
of 'the products of a number of Northern brewers' took place at the
De Grey Rooms close to the meeting. Unlike St Alban's and Cardiff,
it was only open to CAMRA delegates, but more than 1,000 people
are reported to have passed through, enjoying an impressive 440
gallons of ale between them.

What's Brewing's reporting demonstrates how difficult it was
to put together a festival of any ambition at this time. Seven brewers
were able to showcase their wares at the event. *What's Brewing*'s editor,
Michael Hardman, referred to a noticeboard displaying letters from
nine other breweries who turned down the invitation to bring their
beers along too.

John Smith's Tadcaster Brewery, then a Courage subsidiary, were
quoted as saying that they did not participate in local beer exhibitions
'because of the unfortunate circumstances attaching to some of them
in the past'. It's terrifying to ponder this comment, considering the
raucous revelry of the World Beer Show hadn't even happened yet.
Beer festivals were not yet respectable places in the public and
professional consciousness.

Timothy Taylor of Keighley, less than 40 miles away from York, declined as the exhibition was being held 'very well away from our operating area'. This hammers home how difficult it was for organisers to source beer from outside their immediate geographical location at this time. Timothy Taylor's Landlord today is consistently one of the top 10 selling cask ales in the country now, available nationwide.

1974 – Cambridge Beer Festival

It was the Cambridge branch of CAMRA who were the first to run a beer festival over several days for the general public. It was the archetype of the now traditional beer festival model.

That first Cambridge festival, held in August 1974, was run on blind optimism by an organising party of almost complete novices. They had a lucky break in that the previous year a beer tent run on Christ's Pieces during the annual music-led Cambridge Festival had been an 'admitted failure'. Organised by the city council and run by caterers, the opening hours were reportedly unreliable, the beer in

CAMBRIDGE branch chairman Alan Hill secures a cask of beer in his car with the safety belt — before making his passengers sit in the back seat for the long drive back from Dusseldorf to England.

The beer was a gift from the Schumacher Brauerei for the Cam-

The beginning of last month's Cambridge beer festival — an event which saw 37,200 pints of beer, 1,000 pints of cider, half a ton of cheese, 7,000 bread rolls and 4,800 pork pies consumed by more than

10,000 people in 39 hours spread over four days.

The festival was the second organised by the Cambridge branch of CAMRA and now looks firmly established as an annual event.

Coverage of the Cambridge Beer Festival in *What's Brewing*

poor condition, and no glasses were available, just paper cups, so punters couldn't even obtain a pint measure. After some gentle cajoling, the council were relatively open to passing the buck to a passionate band of beer lovers in 1974.

Two of the key members of the CAMRA branch's organising committee were John Bishopp and Chris Bruton, both of whom had worked a few shifts in a pub before. This was the sum total of relevant experience amongst the group. Because of this, they set up the festival as an enormous pub, and kept roughly to pub hours for a number of years until the event got too big. Fortuitously, they discovered that a club in Norwich had been running their own private festival for several years, and were able to tap them up for advice.

The brewers were eventually convinced that there was enough cellar experience on hand to entrust their beers to the team. The landlord of the Queen's Head at Newton, David Short, was a CAMRA member and kindly agreed to hold the licence. He continued to do this until well into the 2000s when a change in the law meant that the licensee needed to be on-site at all times. Since around 2011, the Cambridge festival organiser has also been the licence holder.

The inaugural festival turned out to be more popular than expected – they ran out of beer after the very first day and had to work through the night to collect more.

> Charles Wells sent an emergency dray with around 25 additional firkins at a second's notice. Greene King were in the area and could drop off too, but many beers had to be collected. The head brewers knew we looked after the beer properly and were a serious commercial operation that wouldn't renege on bills! So we had a good reputation; at Cambridge and the festivals that followed.
>
> TONY MILLNS, former CAMRA Chairman
> and Cambridge volunteer

The volunteer staff were also, understandably, overwhelmed.

> Luckily some of the first people through the door were CAMRA members, and they never left. They were bludgeoned into working behind the bars. We had intended to run the festival with about six people!
>
> JOHN BISHOPP, OG Cambridge Beer Festival organisers

Cambridge Beer Festival in the 1980s (photos Robert Flood)

One of the most exciting beers was from the famous Dusseldorf Altbier producer, Schumacher. It had been driven over specially, donated as a favour from some German colleagues of the Cambridge branch chair, Alan Hill. Alan relegated his wife to the back seat for the journey so the barrel could be safely strapped into the front. The taps were turned on during the first day and they weren't turned off until the beer ran out.

Aside from this foreign dignitary, the other beers came from around 10 different breweries all within easy striking distance of Cambridge so that punters could easily find them again.

At the fifth annual festival, there was trouble in store for a friend of the organising committee – one George Abbott who ran a travel agent around the corner. He was always at the festival, generally hiding from his wife I am told. He came in absolutely fuming – he had been featured by the *Cambridge Daily News* and his cover was blown.

There was at least one familiar face at the revels, that owned by Mr George Abbott of Abbott Travel. There's scarcely a watering hole in town that I've been without seeing George sampling the wares. In spite of it all, though, he stays remarkably trim. What, I wondered, is his secret?

"Just a matter of your metabolism," he replied. "I eat and drink as much as I like and it doesn't make any difference." As if to reinforce his point his T-shirt reads: "I've swallowed Abbott." (Cambridge CAMRA chairman John Bishopp also swallows Abbotts but there the similarity ends as our picture shows.)

In recent years the valuable stocks of real ale have been stored in the nearby vaults of the Midland Bank, whether for conditioning or security reasons we don't know. But the practice has now ended, says CAMRA secretary Tony Millns, whose enviable job involves sampling all 34 brews between 9 and 10.30am to ensure their suitability for sale.

"Now we store them around the Corn Exchange," he says. "In the hours we're closed the empty barrels are replaced. When there are only a couple of gallons left in a barrel then we drink it between us. That's so that we can ensure a fresh and full barrel will be in operation for the next session."

And do you know, he said it with his eyes wide so open that
I walked away completely convinced that it was simply one of
those occupational hazards

JOHN GASKELL, *Cambridge Daily News*, Friday 21 July 1978

It hasn't always been plain sailing for the committee. In 1989 the
festival was nearly cancelled due to a lack of organisers, which goes
to show how precarious every local CAMRA festival is. Without a
willing and able committee, year in, year out, these festivals simply
wouldn't happen.

The festival continues to be a great success today, now sited on
Jesus Green. The 2023 festival welcomed 38,000 visitors who enjoyed
72,000 pints of beer and 9,461 pints of cider. More than 850 people
signed up for the Campaign for Real Ale and more than £15,000 was
raised for East Anglia's Children's Hospices.

We got a very wide range of drinkers. One evening, I was at the
front door watching the people coming in and going out. Leaving
the hall were two blokes both dressed in black leather with
assorted piercings and safety-pins – Cambridge was a bit ahead
of the curve on that sort of thing – and I overheard the one with
a purple Mohican say to the one with a green Mohican "I've had
three pints of that Robinson's Old Tom – tastes like Coca-Cola but
takes your fucking head off." Well, I thought, if we can achieve that
sort of broad appeal, we're going to change the country's drinking
habits.   TONY MILLNS, Former CAMRA Chairman
and Cambridge volunteer

1975 – Covent Garden is alive with real ale

People living in Covent Garden – which is probably the last
village community in central London – are enthusiastic about
the festival and have been helping CAMRA in an attempt to
keep the area alive.   *What's Brewing*, September 1975

John Bishopp and Chris Bruton wrote up the formula they had used to
develop the Cambridge festival and gave it to CAMRA headquarters.
Thus they inadvertently volunteered themselves as organisers for the
first national CAMRA festival in Covent Garden that was held a year

Coverage of the Covent Garden Beer Festival in *What's Brewing*

later, on 9th to 13th September 1975. Their template included items like a Wednesday to Saturday schedule and a trade afternoon at the start of the festival, and these are still commonplace across CAMRA festivals of all sizes today.

One of the most challenging aspects was finding a suitable venue. Negotiations with Camden Lock fell through, which is a shame as some of the beer would have been delivered by barge. Issues with fire regulations prevented the event from being staged at St Katherine's Dock near the Tower of London. It wasn't until July 1975 that negotiations with the disused Covent Garden Flower Market were announced. The empty market was not in a great state, but perfect to hold a festival, with the flower stalls still intact and making excellent stillaging for the beer.

> A number of problems still need to be ironed out – mainly involving the cleaning of the building, electricity supply and fire regulations – but the CAMRA team of John Bishopp, Chris Bruton and Eric Spragett are optimistic about the prospects of the festival going ahead.
>
> *What's Brewing*, July 1975

Once permission was obtained from the Greater London Council to use the old flower market rent-free, there was an ambition for the festival to act as the forerunner of a much bigger, annual event. The seeds of the Great British Beer Festival had been sown.

Eric Spragett was CAMRA's Commercial Manager and he organised the refurbishment of the space. This included installing a power supply and building toilets. Unfortunately, he may not have done the best job in this regard, as some customers reportedly preferred to urinate in a corner of the hall rather than use them.

There were a number of unusual challenges, not least the whole area being closed down by the police on the first day that the crew had access to set up the building. The team had decamped to the Young's pub across the road at close of play for a welcome pint, almost certainly the Marquess of Anglesey on Bow Street. John Bishopp picks up the story:

> Having been working south of London that morning, I'd left my briefcase in the office and gone to join the crew that were starting the set up. When we'd finished in the flower market, I'd asked Gill [Keay – a fellow member of the organising committee] if she would be so kind as to bring my briefcase across, because she was going to go and close the office up. I must admit, having asked her, we went across to the pub and I had completely forgotten about it.

> Somebody came into the pub and said "do you know, the whole of that part of London is closed down because of a bomb scare?" And I don't know how, but I suddenly thought "where the hell is my briefcase?" and somebody else went white faced and dashed out of the pub, came back and said "you've got to go to Bow Street police station and claim your briefcase".

> What had happened is that Gill had picked the briefcase up, taken it out of Henrietta Street, put it down beside her to lock the door, completely forgotten that she'd got a briefcase with her and walked away without it. And it was only the fact, so the police told me, that there was a "Covent Garden is Alive with Real Ale" sticker on the front of the briefcase that they didn't put a round through it. Which would have destroyed the briefcase and a very expensive book that was inside. So, although I hadn't left the briefcase, it was me that had to go back and claim it! And face what turned out to be not the wrath of Bow Street. They were very good about it.

> In fact it then paid us back in dividends, although it was a very unfortunate incident. We had Bow Street police station look after us extremely well throughout the whole of the festival.

We never, ever argued when an off-duty policeman came up
to the door and flashed a warrant card. He was let in in front
of all the people that were queuing.

They were a great help, certainly in the management of
the crowds outside. But I think we were more worried about
Man United supporters on the Saturday than terrorists.

JOHN BISHOPP, festival organiser

The licence to sell alcohol wasn't in place until the morning of
the festival. A local landlord had been lined up to obtain it, but he
pulled out at the last minute thanks to pressure from neighbouring
licensees. In the end, it was Anthony Ansell, the Marketing Director
at Fuller's Brewery, who came to the rescue. He was at the court
getting the necessary papers at 10.30am when the festival was due
to open at midday.

Real ale fans mingled with smart suits from the City to enjoy
the most British beer that had ever been brought together in one place
before. Of the 75 UK breweries in 1975, 30 were represented at the
festival, including the Laird of Traquair House hand-delivering his
bottled beer.

The beer that created the most interest was, perhaps,
Pollard's bitter from Reddish, near Stockport, which has only
recently been introduced. David Pollard, the brewer, was at
the festival to see his beer snapped up literally within hours.

Pollard's beer created a great deal of interest at a Press
reception before the festival opened and his small stand
was surrounded by reporters and cameramen for hours.

What's Brewing, October 1975

For those who fancied a change from Pollard's bitter, there were
plenty of other options on hand. 'The barrels (actually firkins) were
racked-up on the cast iron flower stalls. At the end of one of these
stalls was a lone water tap. Above the tap was a blackboard on which
some wag had chalked "WATNEYS ON DRAUGHT" with an
arrow pointing to the tap.' (Peter G Scott, CAMRA member.)

Some 150,000 pints were consumed across the four-day festival.
Around 200 CAMRA members selflessly volunteered their time to
run the festival, which was widely considered a success. However,

with such a large event, there were teething troubles and not everyone was happy.

More than 40,000 people visited the festival during its five days and 400-yard-long queues formed outside the market well after the doors were opened for each session. The arrangements for issuing beer tokens and glasses could not cope with the unexpected demand and a number of people queued for hours without getting in.

A number of complaints about the organisation of the festival were received at CAMRA Headquarters but one of the organisers said later: "We were knocked out by the number of people who wanted to sample the 50 brews available. Only a few days before the festival began we did not know whether the hall would be packed, half full or empty. We even thought at one stage that we might make a loss." From the moment the doors first opened, however, it was obvious that the organisers had completely underestimated the demand. All 15,000 souvenir glasses were snapped up by the second day and plastic glasses had to be hurriedly brought in. Emergency supplies of beer also had to be arranged – with deliveries coming from as far as the Belhaven brewery in Scotland. It is not yet known exactly how much profit the festival made, but it is certainly in excess of £5,000.

The event was staffed almost completely by volunteers who had given up their spare time to sell tokens, glasses, beer, food, CAMRA products, guides and membership. The only paid staff were from a security firm who were called in to man the exits following an outbreak of terrorist bombing in London the week before the festival began.   *What's Brewing*, October 1975

One disgruntled CAMRA member was forthright in expressing his grievances at not getting into the festival: 'There is an old Army saying to describe extreme incompetence: "He couldn't organise a piss-up in a brewery." I am disappointed to have to report that CAMRA qualified for this description at Covent Garden.'

JC TURNER, Pevensey, writing to *What's Brewing*, November 1975

From a campaigning perspective, the event was a huge win. Hundreds of people signed up for CAMRA membership at Covent

Garden. Chris Holmes, who would become CAMRA Chairman in 1976, even signed up the English novelist Sir Kingsley Amis.

However, a break in at CAMRA HQ in St Albans diminished the celebratory mood. Along with £900 in cash and £300 in cheques, some 500 applications for membership were stolen before the information had been entered into the membership files. A press release went out to local papers around the country appealing to those members to get in touch so that they could be put on file to receive their membership perks.

Beer festivals have always been critical in bringing new members to the Campaign for Real Ale. This is no different today than it was 50 years ago.

> While it's not an experiment we would have wanted to conduct, COVID and the lockdowns did very clearly show how important festivals are to CAMRA in driving recruitment. With retention remaining more or less the same, the main factor which changed between 2019 and 2020 was our ability to run festivals, and it had a dramatic effect on recruitment numbers. In recent years, as festivals have slowly started up again, we've seen the positive effect this has had on recruitment.
>
> Festivals remain hugely important for CAMRA in terms of recruitment. They're an opportunity for us to speak to a large number of non-members, who already have an interest in beer, and tell them about the benefits membership brings. Our festivals are a very clear demonstration of our campaigning, and the social and volunteering opportunities being a member offers.
>
> TOM STAINER, CAMRA Chief Executive

How to Run a Beer Festival

Cambridge, and then Covent Garden, gave the network of CAMRA branches a template by which festivals could be organised. That template came with the offer of some equipment that was needed to build the festival bars themselves, available to other CAMRA branches wishing to run their own festival. 'We started building up a stock of everything needed to run a beer festival – from taps and chocks to bar counters – quite early on. Quite a lot of the kit spent most of the 1980s in the garage at my house in Cyprus Road, where folk like John and Chris Cryne would come and collect what they needed to run the Bedford Beer Festival, for instance.' (Tony Millns, former CAMRA Chairman.)

Cambridge Branch Treasurer, John Abraham, had really got stuck into the logistics for the first Cambridge Beer Festival in 1974 by making bar counters out of plywood sheets with blockboard counter-tops at his home, with about 15 other branch members forming a production line. They had hinged front and side panels so that they could be stored flat and John suspects that some of them may still be in use at festivals around the country to this day.

Making and storing equipment at home could only be viable for so long – not least for the health and safety and insurance ramifica-tions. The pool of kit came to reside with CAMRA headquarters in St Albans, with official procedures put in place for borrowing, asses-sing and returning items.

> I joined CAMRA and went to my first festival in the late 1970s. I think my first festival was a Great British Beer Festival at Alexandra Palace in '78 or '79. I went to festivals as a customer on a regular basis. I was made redundant in 2008, so volunteered for the [Pig's Ear] festival for the first time. I duly turned up on the first day of the set-up period and was bemused to be told to go and get in a cab outside because I was going to St Albans. It turned out we get most of our equipment from the HQ warehouse there. We had to go and collect at that time; they deliver these days.
>
> STEVE HALL, Pig's Ear festival organiser

Most festivals require a forklift truck to get everything into place. The Great British Beer Festival now needs a small fleet of such vehicles to tackle the massive logistical challenge of getting hundreds of casks racked on the stillage. Sarah Durham worked on beer ordering for many years, and remembers that one year, with Olympia's permission, they used a forklift to move a car that had been parked by people using another part of the venue. It was blocking the access for all of their deliveries so had to be put out of the way.

*   *   *

I wanted to get a feel for the process of organising a CAMRA beer festival, so I went along to the inaugural meeting of the Bridgnorth 2024 Festival Committee. It was held at the Railwayman's Arms in the town, a cracking little boozer crammed full of railway memorabilia situated on platform 1 of the historic Severn Valley Railway station. This was a fitting location, since the festival itself is held at the station and has been since it began in 1995. You can watch a great little video of the set-up and the festival itself made by Dave Haddon on YouTube, just search for '1995 CAMRA / Severn Valley Railway Beer Festival'. That shows how volunteers put a beer festival together perhaps better than I have space to describe it here!

Anyway, back to the meeting. Everyone was pleased to have around 20 faces around the table. Bridgnorth CAMRA is a sub-branch of Telford and East Shropshire, and, worried that they could no longer provide enough volunteers to run the festival alone, they had appealed to the main branch for more support. Telford Chair Graham Sarbutt had stepped into the role of festival organiser, ably assisted by the Events Officer, Paul Jones. In combination with a few experienced pairs of hands (some of whom can be seen in that 1995 video I mentioned) there was a sense of strong optimism that the festival could be expected not just to survive, but to thrive.

The main business of the meeting was to allocate key roles so that the organisation of the festival could swing into action. A comprehensive business plan had already been approved by CAMRA HQ so all the key details were already in place. Beer ordering, festival glasses and hire of the marquee were also discussed, along with sponsorship, power, food and cooling.

The building blocks of the festival were all put into place to the satisfaction of all present with six months to go until the event took off. Bridgnorth is certainly at the smaller end of the CAMRA beer festival family, but the wonderfully picturesque location makes it the envy of many. And, for reasons I cannot yet fathom, I volunteered to help with the marketing. It's hard not to get drawn into the enthusiasm of beer lovers, talking about beer.

Beer Quality

> Half the time it was the brewers setting up the beer festivals with the CAMRA members, and everyone was part of the same team, at the early festivals.　　KEITH BOTT, Titanic Brewery

At the heart of every great festival, there must be fantastic beer. While contemporary craft beer festivals rely predominantly on kegged beers, which are just plug-and-play, cask beer requires a lot more skill to serve in good condition. If this hadn't been a key priority of CAMRA festivals from day one, they would never have lasted. The support of the brewers was vital in the early days to help inexperienced volunteers learn the ropes, although there were plenty of former publicans and brewers who were CAMRA members themselves on hand too to help get everyone trained up.

> It's a live beer, so in the cask it's still working away. You have to get the beer from the dray onto the stillage as soon as you can. Especially the stronger beers because they take longer to settle down and for the yeast to form at the bottom of the cask.
>
> Once you've rested it for, say 12 to 24 hours, you need to vent them and give them a little while for some air to get into the cask. You don't want too much, because as soon as the air hits the beer you're on a timer [before it spoils]. And then you tap it. And then it's in the lap of the gods.

A Peterborough volunteer checks quality (left); Pig's Ear cellar team members Pete Large and Derek Jones

It all depends on the room temperature. The colder it is, the longer it will take for the flavours of the beer to come through. We used to have some heat blasters outside [at the historic Round Chapel, Hackney] to bring up the whole building to a normal, ambient temperature. The cold was stopping them from maturing, if you like.

You're looking at all this year on year, looking at what has changed. How can you overcome problems? It's absolutely essential that all of us were trained by a number of other people. Like anything in life, you learn from the experiences of others.

DEREK JONES, Pig's Ear Festival cellar team, London

There are a huge number of parameters to take into consideration when dealing with cask ale, as former Fuller's head brewer, John Keeling, explains:

I always thought ESB was best in the third week of its life. But a festival just has to take it as it is. Some beers drop bright in 24 hours, some take 48 hours. And little things happen at festivals. Suddenly they have to move things because there's an emergency – and you shouldn't move cask beer on a stillage. Or the beer doesn't get delivered in time, that's a big problem.

With cask it's particularly tricky. But with CAMRA festivals you would have the same people who would do it every year and they built up experience. They knew what they were doing. But even with people of experience, you still have problems. So with Fuller's, it is never soft spiled, it is hard spiled. If we were in a festival in Leeds and they soft spiled London Pride, it was not in as good a condition. That would make it go flatter, quicker.

JOHN KEELING, Former Fuller's Head Brewer

Iain Loe, of the Avon Branch, recalls his earliest festival experiences, and the importance of knowing the character of each beer.

One of the first festivals I was involved in was in Bristol at the old Watershed buildings before they became all gentrified. It was the Great Western Beer Festival that the Avon Branch of CAMRA ran. I remember all these beers suddenly arriving, many of which were in an unfined form. We had a local licensee coming in and opening the shive, pouring in a pint or two of finings, tapping it back in and rolling it around. And then humping it up onto scaffolding, since there were no electric lifts or anything at the time. We spiled them and you'd see the spouts of beer shooting out because a lot of these beers that we had were lively.

Probably the most lively of all were the beers from the Penrhos Brewery which the late Terry Jones had set up. They came in wooden casks, they tended to be 18s [a kilderkin] so they were difficult to handle. When you spiled them they certainly bubbled for a long time but when they settled down they were actually excellent in taste. It was that hands-on experience in the early days of campaigning that I really found enjoyable.

IAIN LOE, Former Chairman of Avon Branch

And of course, with each festival being unique and each set up being built from scratch, a fair amount of bodging is necessary to make sure the show goes on. 'Problem. The 300 brass taps from Tetleys are not designed for gravity serving. Brian Dummons concocts an addition to the design from old egg boxes and a couple of Fairy Liquid bottles. No problem.' (Tim Webb writing a light-hearted festival organisers Diary for *What's Brewing* after GBBF 1982.)

It can't be said that every festival gets it right. There are often moans and groans about the beers' condition. One disgruntled punter took up his pen to wax lyrical on the subject to the *Staffordshire Sentinel* in 1989. He was responding to columnist Alan Cookman's review of the ninth Stoke festival from the previous week, although it should be noted that Mr Cookman was quite clear that he wasn't denigrating the condition of the beers. Those that Alan memorably found to be 'unutterably disgusting' were simply not to his personal taste, not 'fundamentally unfit for human consumption'.

Myself and up to 10 other dedicated drinkers attend this function every year and agree it is well run and a great success. However, we all find the quality of the beer to be at best 50 percent good, 50 percent poor or bad.

The problem with some real ale boffins is that they reckon that anything that comes out of a handpump is superior. Not so.

It all needs looking after to varying degrees and, of course, some doesn't travel well. This is the primary reason why lager drinkers shun real ale because while you may always get a bland brew, at least you don't get a vinegary concoction as with an "off" bitter.

'Life-long bitter drinker', *Staffordshire Sentinel*, Thursday, 9 November 1989

And of course, even when quality levels are excellent, you still might not taste what you are expecting. 'I went to the 2006 Pig's Ear Festival, the first at the Ocean, as a customer. The casks were haphazardly organised, and the beer lines resembled a plate of spaghetti. When you asked for a specific beer the reply was usually "I am not sure which one that is" – and you got served something different.' (Steve Hall, Pig's Ear festival organiser [but not in 2006].)

Cask Cooling

Speaking with festival organisers up and down the country, temperature control is their single biggest issue. At the first festival in Cambridge, they covered the casks with layers of hessian sacking that were castoffs from the building firm one of the members worked for. They used a garden sprayer to moisten them with water every hour or two. Since this hessian was 'pre-loved' for keeping concrete damp while it cured, this wasn't perhaps the most hygienic option.

Hessian sacking was also used at the Great British Beer Festival in 1980, which was held under canvas after the fire destroyed the Alexandra Palace. Three refrigerated trailers hired through Truman's also kept the beer in good condition, along with ten tons of ice which was placed on the sack-covered casks.

The Robin Hood Beer & Cider Festival had the benefit of holding their event on the covered ice rink of the Nottingham Ice Arena in 2018 and 2019. Good temperature stability guaranteed! But Nottingham has form when it comes to innovative solutions for cask cooling.

Before 2008, we were at the old Victorian swimming baths. They've been knocked down now. We had the old swimming pool floored over for the festival and we did have a problem with cooling. We used towels on the casks, and invented a system where there was a hose permanently running along the top with holes poked in it and so the towels were always wet. Because it was a swimming baths it didn't matter because the water just drained away.

And even before the Victoria Baths, we once built a structure out of canvas, effectively like a paddling pool that did the same thing, water the casks. We put a handpump on this thing so we could pump the water out of it. We put a Greene King IPA pumpclip on it.

STEVE WESTBY, Chairman of Nottingham CAMRA, and Robin Hood Beer & Cider festival organiser

Alan Thwaites keeps an eye on quality at Bridgnorth

Casks rest on the stillage in their cooling jackets

These days the casks all rest comfortably in padded jackets that are fed by a flow of water from an in-line cooling system, thanks to the stock of equipment held centrally by CAMRA. Wet cloths are now optional, though still often seen, but a fair amount of running repairs and ad hoc innovation is still required to keep things operational.

One GBBF bar manager once had a leak in their cooling set-up so the night team had to put down a huge amount of 'kitty litter' down – green absorbent Pyrasorb granules. It earned the bar the nickname of 'the putting green'.

A lot of the cooling equipment was originally constructed by volunteers when Christine Cryne first introduced a cooling system at the Great British Beer Festival in 1992. It has had heavy maintenance over the years and volunteers every year descend on the warehouse to do the upkeep. 'I first attended one of these "cooling weekends" in 2008 and have been to many. They are always a fun occasion, a place to catch up with fellow volunteers along with sampling some beer from the local pubs! These weekends we both maintain equipment and construct new ones such as the "pythons" used at GBBF ensuring beer is cooled all the way from the cask to your glass.' (Catherine Tonry, GBBF festival organiser 2018–2024.)

On the whole, beer quality is rarely an issue these days, thanks to the equipment and the commitment of the cellar team. I can't express the magnitude of the work they do better than Laura Emson, a CAMRA National Director and serial festival volunteer. She wrote this on her own Instagram feed:

> It's hard to explain the mindset of volunteering at a CAMRA beer festival especially in the cellar/cooling team. We're on site days before the festival opens. We're in before anyone else in the morning and working well after the last customer has left the building. The morning after everything closes we're there clearing up. It's hard work, mentally and physically, we get wet from water and beer, we're usually on the floor or climbing over casks, and the laundry takes a good few days after to work through. We build a pub from scratch and break it back down again, but this is not IKEA flat pack. Every festival is unique – quirky buildings and their custodians, indoors and out, a few casks over a day or hundreds over a week. We can't call technical services to fix our leaks – we are technical services! All we have to make beer flow again or keep it cool is our kit, what can be bought on a typical high street, and buckets of ingenuity. There's no manual and all our training comes from other volunteers. In turn we train those keen to learn and enjoy watching them figure out this giant plumbing Meccano set for themselves. For me, recovering from burnout and living with ADHD, there are times when it gets overwhelming. That's when the team pick me up, keep me fed, and leave me to figure it out for myself. People I've just met or have known for years, from all walks of life, living in places hundreds of miles from me, but to them I'm a part of their festival. It's a privilege to be accepted and have my skills valued and enhanced by these festivals.
>
> LAURA EMSON, writing on Instagram in June 2024

The Tale of the Exploding Cask

No matter which festival I go to, someone always has a story of a vented cask spurting beer across incredible distances. Here are a few choice anecdotes (whittled down from hundreds).

Nottingham

'The Victorian swimming baths had a very high ceiling. Natural light came through the glass ceiling at the top of high walls. I vented a Timothy Taylors Ram Tam and the jet that came out of it actually hit the ceiling. That was some hell of a distance. And that mark stayed on that ceiling. It was still there for every year afterwards until they knocked the place down! I think the thing with Ram Tam was, so they say, it was Landlord with caramel added. They call it Landlord Dark now, I think.

'I was hammering a tap into a kil [kilderkin]. It had been vented but the tap shot out across the room. And the beer was just spurting out. I grabbed a clean tap and I had to run at the jet and force the clean tap back into it and hit it with a hammer very quickly. Needless to say I was absolutely soaked. We bring a clean set of clothes, because you do get accidents.'

STEVE WESTBY, Chair of Nottingham CAMRA
Robin Hood Beer and Cider Festival organiser

Pig's Ear

'Pete Large and I, we were in Stratford at the Old Town Hall. We had this beer that was notorious for being lively. It was Sarah's Hop House, Black Mamba Mild. We had vented it, but we knew it was quite volatile in the cask, so instead of doing what we normally do, vent it with a wooden spile, we thought we would use a specific venting tool that's got an outlet on it.

'It seemed to settle down. Pete said "Well, it seems to be all right now." He loosened the spile at the top and started to tap it. He broke the seal and all we heard was this WHOOOSH!

'That went over my shoulder and there was beer all over me and a couple of people behind as well! It was the most difficult beer that I've ever had to deal with. Apparently, it hit the ceiling in Stratford Town

Hall. I'm not sure I should say this, but after the festival they actually got some people in because they thought they'd got some sort of dry rot in the ceiling.

'The upshot was when it eventually settled down and we could actually stop the flow, out of nine gallons we had three gallons left.'

DEREK JONES, Pig's Ear Festival cellar team, London

Skipton

'The beer was in the annex. It was fortunate we had made this decision as our beer-ordering guru had the bright idea of ordering a strawberry beer. This was just a bit lively and, when an inexperienced volunteer tapped it, there was a lot of swearing as the beer hit the ceiling, and sprayed into the bar manager's face. (We never did find out which upset her most.) Had we been in the main hall, it might have brought all the crumbling plaster down! As it was, it just left a red stain on the ceiling. (Don't tell the Town Hall Manager!) Our bar manager now has a strange aversion to fruit beers.'

Skipton Beer Festival 2008, taken from the festival website

Canterbury

'We used to keep the beer cool with wet roller towels, but after one year when we set up in 37-degree heat, we switched to using CAMRA's coolers, especially as a cask of raspberry wheat beer blew out its shive and showered the bar with a mush of real raspberries.'

GILL KEAY, Canterbury festival organiser for 40 years

Logistics

Glasses

Even when the beer is in good condition on the stillage, there's still a lot of work to do to run a festival. First off, guests need something to drink their beer from. Glasses have been a perpetual headache for CAMRA organising committees. Ordering pint pots with bespoke logos is an additional expense to consider, and since the festival is organised by volunteers, they rarely have any storage available, so visitors are encouraged to take their glasses away. This fact has taken a surprisingly long time to sink into the national consciousness.

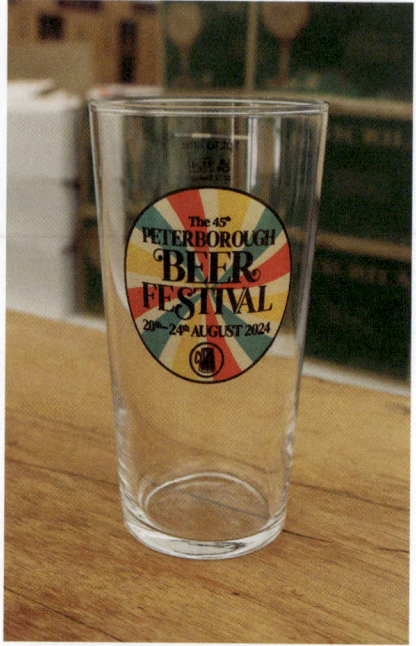

Glasses from a range of festivals

Primary school teacher and festival organiser Chris Cobbold told me: "We had more than 1,500 people through those doors last year. Trouble? Not even a hint of it. A couple of policemen wandered in one night, but only to ask if we knew the punters were stealing our glasses. We explained that visitors pay £1 deposit for their glasses and are welcome to take them away as souvenirs if they don't want their money back."

"'That's all right then,'" said the officers, and went on their way."

Danny Blyth stood me a glass of cherry beer and said past reports of disorderly conduct at CAMRA beer festivals had been greatly exaggerated. "Since CAMRA was founded, back in 1971, there have only been three arrests at our festivals – a pickpocket up north somewhere and a couple nicked for committing an indecent act in public in Blackpool."

JULIE HEARN, writing about the Wimbledon Beer Festival for the *Kingston Informer*, Friday 11 March 1988

Once festival-goers were leaving, glass in hand, the next step was to give them a bag to put it in to stop them waltzing around the streets with open containers of alcohol.

When we held our first ever festival in Aberdeen [September 1987] in a magnificent music hall with mahogany walls, the Cowdray Hall, the glass supplier offered to deliver to Dundee – 80 miles away! We finally got them to deliver on site.

It's a simple process. You come in the door, you pay your admission, you get to keep your glass. We don't want your glasses back because we've got nowhere to put them. But on the Saturday we got a call from the police:

"We've had all these people walking round from your festival with stolen glasses."

"No, they're their glasses!"

"Oh, well, we took them off them ..."

Part of the reason was that they were walking around the streets with the glass in their hand. So next festival, we made sure everyone's got a bag to put their glasses in.

TERRY LOCK, former CAMRA National Executive member

But what sort of glass do you get? As a consumer organisation, CAMRA has long campaigned for full measures – a full pint of liquid not including the head of the beer. As part of this campaign, the use of oversized, lined glasses was enshrined in policy for all CAMRA beer festivals from 1992.

At first, those lines showed the pint and half pint measure. The next natural evolution was the introduction of the third pint line, as well as dedicated third-pint glasses. They had enjoyed a bit of a revival in pubs as a taster glass, which the *Morning Advertiser* reported on in 2001.

Third glasses were offered at GBBF in 2006, and reportedly sold out because they were so popular. It made sense for the consumer organisation to give customers the opportunity to try a wide range of beers in smaller quantities – enjoying variety while drinking responsibly. The third line was inscribed on the GBBF pint glass the next year, in 2007, and has remained there ever since.

Beer Tokens

Buying a drink isn't a complicated transaction, but CAMRA have come up with a variety of systems for how people pay for their beer at a festival. One of the key drivers is to minimise the amount of cash handling expected of volunteers working on the bar. Tokens were available from a separate desk as far back as the 1975 national festival in Covent Garden, where cash amounts could be marked off as they were spent.

Crossing out the value of a drink

However, even marking off the correct amount and keeping an eye on the felt tip pen slows down bar volunteers to some extent – not ideal at peak times during service. A new token system was devised in the early 2000s and named after the branch that devised it – the Nottingham system.

Two tokens buy a third, and three purchase a half for most cask ales. Stronger beers cost more tokens, reflecting their higher purchase price. Unused tokens can easily be refunded when a customer leaves the session, or the value donated to charity.

The rise of the cashless society has meant that many festivals now simply have card readers at the bar which are easy for volunteers and customers to use. However, in recognition that some people still hold cash as king, some festivals operate a hybrid system. At the Wolverhampton Beer & Cider Festival 2024, for example, the old-style cash amount cards were available for purchase by cash or card as well as contactless payment being offered on the bar. This worked relatively seamlessly and seemed to suit all comers.

Food

When people have access to a lot of interesting beer, it's a good idea to put a bit of grub out for them as well. Traditional pub snacks are naturally the most common at beer festivals; the great beige British buffet of sausage rolls, scotch eggs, pork pies and filled cobs. When asked about festivals, food is often one of the first things people mention.

Festival food at GBBF

Street food at GBBF Winter 2020 in Birmingham

'I remember in particular the very fine beers from the local Milton Brewery. In particular Pegasus which was lovely. It was always a very well organised festival in a nice situation on Jesus Green. They did a good scotch egg and sausage roll as I recall.' (Toby Crooks, Cambridge festival gourmand in the early 2000s.)

Toby is right to get hung up on the dining options. The Cambridge beer festival has always taken pride in the quality it offers, as this press release in the local paper from 1981 shows.

And the food will be as good as ever. (I was recently asked by an outside company for the name of our caterers as they had heard they were the best in the business. They were particularly saddened when I informed them we did it ourselves). The secret, of course, is the ingredients. Only the best will be on show: local baked granary bread, farmhouse cheeses, like the beer, it hasn't been processed and pasteurised, Cambridge pork pies and baked hams, and home-baked flans. All this will be on sale at reasonable prices.

Cambridge Daily News, Tuesday, 21 July 1981

There are often local specialities available to try. For many years the Leicester beer festival, when held at the Charotar Patidar Samaj, was rightly known for its superlative curries.

If you were lucky at the Nottingham Beer Festival over the years, you might have spotted Dave Bartram, the Cockle Man. Dave has been wielding his basket of fishy delights around city pubs since 1965. Such is his fame, his regular number 10 bus was named after him by Nottingham City Transport in 2019.

At its height, his business had seven staff and served 250 pubs, but he says the smoking ban and the rise of the chain pub has hurt his trade. He has also courted controversy by adding peperamis to his basket, but he defended the decision, saying it was what the punters wanted. A true local institution, the Cockle Man celebrated his 80th birthday in 2024 and is starting to think about retirement, although he certainly walked the festival floor in 2023.

While some early CAMRA festivals were ambitiously providing the food themselves, many sought the support of local caterers. Indeed, some venues insisted on it. Denis Palmer remembers Ginsters 'featuring strongly in the early years.' The family-run pasty business in Cornwall was bought by the Midlands based Samworth Brothers when Geoffrey Ginster retired in 1977.

Gill Keay ran the food service at Covent Garden in 1975 ('mainly bread and cheese and pork pies'). While the Great British Beer Festival went on to have caterers who serviced the public, the organisers put on the staff food themselves. In 1978, she remembers making a carbonnade – a Flemish beef stew with Truman's beer – but the bank of borrowed microwaves weren't up to the task of making the baked potatoes to go with it, so they had to outsource the job to the homes of local CAMRA members. The community comes through once again! 'I remember that we all got breakfast at Ally Pally, served by a holy terror from their staff, Edie. It was a pleasure to see her berate CAMRA Chair Chris Bruton. Not so much of a pleasure to cope with her idea of heating up the tinned tomatoes – stone cold but on a red hot plate.' (Gill Keay, CAMRA Festival Legend for 50 years.)

Gill was recorded in action once again at the 1982 GBBF in Leeds, selling nearly 300 gallons of mushy peas, thousands of hot pork pies and half a kilo of mint sauce.

But Cambridge makes a bold pitch for the title of Best Staff Food (and most interesting sounding 1970s parties). 'We tried in a rather John Lewis sort of way to make sure the volunteer staff had a good time – and the Sunday evening parties after we'd closed and taken all the scaffolding down became legendary for their food (I used to roast a 20lb joint of beef), free beer and the injuries caused by drunken roller-skating round the Corn Exchange.' (John Bishopp, one of the first Cambridge festival organisers.)

The incredible proliferation of talented mobile street food vendors that the UK has enjoyed over the past 20 years has made it easier than ever before for beer festivals to offer culinary quality that matches the standard of the beer.

Entertainment

The character of a beer festival is often shaped not just by the drinks list, but by the entertainment it provides. There is something very special about attending a festival at Burton-upon-Trent's Town Hall, for example, and hearing the jolly tones of their renowned Wurlitzer organ belting out – something I particularly enjoyed at the Great British Beer Festival Winter in February 2024.

'We like the beer as well, but this is the main reason for our visit,' Ronald and Hannah Wheatley told the *Burton Daily Mail* in September 1994. Aged 84 and 79, they were visiting the opening ceremony of Burton's 15th annual festival.

In one festival a Wurlitzer, an acoustic stage at another, a brass band at one more. But festival entertainment is about much more than just music. In the early days, many games were offered, often with a 'school sports day' feel to them. The first Peterborough Beer Festival in 1978 included a welly-wanging competition and a tug-of-war, for example.

Of course, drinking a yard of ale is less often seen on sports day, but it certainly had its place at beer festivals of the 70s and 80s. I'll go out on a limb and say that yard drinking is less common now because society at large is less convinced that downing 2.4 pints in one go is A Good Idea. Still, it makes a good story.

I think it was either the first or second Pig's Ear festival we decided to try a yard of ale. It was funny watching these people stood in a kiddie's paddling pool trying to drink it, everybody else cheering them on. But they didn't know you have to twist it. They drank the first bit and were thinking "where's the rest of it" and all of a sudden – WHOOSH! Without the paddling pool it would've made a hell of a mess.

PETE LARGE, Cellar Emeritus at the Pig's Ear festival

Some entertainments never seem to have quite caught on, despite being undeniably imaginative in nature. The 1980 Loughborough Beer Festival featured fruit machines and video games at the Loughborough Town Hall, with all proceeds being donated to local charities. Perhaps video games don't have enough of a social element for the idea to have caught on.

In 1995 the North Pole pub in Wateringbury, Kent held an English beer and American food festival. Alongside the yard of ale drinking competition, there was a more questionable tobacco-spitting contest. There is no record of the event being reprised in 1996.

Since even before CAMRA existed, the popularity of Oktoberfest-inspired beer festivals has kept many an oompah band in gainful employment. Twelve of the first 13 annual festivals in Derby featured these jolly tones, but the local branch magazine recorded how the 14th would not be so welcoming.

The axing of this highly popular entertainment has been caused by the disgusting behaviour of a minority of louts who thought that throwing beer around was good fun last year.

The stupid behaviour became so bad on the Saturday evening of the 1990 Festival that decent folk could not enjoy themselves, and many left, dripping, in disgust.

Derby Drinker, issue 38, July 1991

It is noticeable, when looking through the archive material, that beer festivals are rarely hotbeds of disorder, so this oompah-inspired upset was a notable outlier.

'We do not want these beer-throwing prats at the Festival again – ever,' said festival Chairman Ivor Clissold, although he was quick to emphasise that it was not the fault of the band. It is clear that CAMRA festivals are dedicated to good clean fun and people who cross the line will not be tolerated.

One entertainment that is synonymous with the beer festival is the seemingly mandatory Morris side. Not all cask ale drinkers are Morris dancers, but it is a truth universally acknowledged that all Morris dancers are cask ale drinkers. I will not be taking further questions on the subject.

They're such a common sight at festivals that the only time I have been caught unawares by Morris was the 2022 Oud Bruin Fest in Kortrijk, Belgium. Sticks and hankies were the last thing I expected to see there, but the Ewell St Mary's Morris Men from the Cotswolds demonstrated that they are more tenacious than the Spanish Inquisition as they danced out to perform in the midst of the Continental wild

The Ewell St Mary's Morris Men perform for the Oud Bruin Fest 2022

beer extravaganza. The gathered crowd was amused and bemused –
to them Morris dancing was clearly quite the novelty. And for reasons
that still remain something of a mystery to me, I ended up chaperoning
most of the group safely back to their hotel, despite only having been
in Kortrijk for a couple of hours myself.

I suspect my experience was less of a shock than the residents of
Horsington in Lincolnshire got when the Elder Tree pub and village
hall held the locality's first beer festival in 1995. The *Horncastle News*
reported that the event was made memorable by the performance of
Irish folk band Shamus O'Blivion and the Megadeath Morris Men,
whose music 'was appreciated some distance from the village hall'.
Shamus and his motley crew are still serving up high-powered folk
rock at beer and music festivals around the land. They even hand out
decorated broom handles at gigs sometimes, in case you haven't
brought your own 'Shamus Stick' to dance with.

In the name of good order, some festivals now shy away from
paying their acts in beer – and with good reason. 'A local bus company
sponsored a brass band to play and in their wisdom the festival
committee had decided to give them free beer tokens as payment.
And the brass band set up around a nine of Lee's Moonraker [a 6.5%
strong ale] and it's possibly the worst brass band you've ever heard
play. It was absolutely hilarious, they were all absolutely battered.'
(Keith Bott, Titanic Brewery.)

*   *   *

Beer festivals have played an important role in the preservation and
revival of traditional pub games. The early pioneer in this sphere was
Timothy Finn, who began researching pub games in the mid-sixties
before publishing the seminal book on the subject in 1966, updated in
1981. In that year he exhibited a selection of games at the Cambridge
Beer Festival to promote his book. His work was eventually built upon
by enthusiastic CAMRA members, who gradually perfected their own
version of the tombola.

An official group was set up in 1985, then known as CAMRA
Fundraising, but now the Games and Collectables Committee, to help
boost festival entertainment and raise funds for the Campaign. 'We put
the fun into the festival,' boasts Pig's Ear Festival Games Manager,

59

Pete Giles. Mick Slaughter was one of the group's founding members.

I had run some small tombola stalls at church events. I went on to run a similar sized stall with just over 100 prizes at a Northampton Beer Festival in 1979. It sold out quickly and so I realised a beer festival stall needed to be much bigger.

Most tombolas run on the basis of picking a raffle ticket out and if it's got a zero or a five at the end, then you're a winner. I tried something slightly different. I worked out that in a raffle ticket book of a thousand tickets, 271 have a figure one in them so the catchphrase was Every 1s A Winner.

The trade secret here is that to get the odds right, you have to use both of the cloakroom tickets for the losers, then there's 271 winners against 1458 losers and the odds are just over five to one. And that means that people get a very good chance to win. We tried to sell tickets in lots of five. We may have sold them at 20p each, but we always said £1 for a strip of five tickets. The reason was that if you picked up five tickets, then there's a good chance you would have a winner.

MICK SLAUGHTER, CAMRA Fundraising

Chancing your arm, Leicester Beer Festival 2020

The festival games at Peterborough Beer Festival

The Every 1s A Winner tombola is a familiar sight at CAMRA festivals these days, with a bell being rung, or the stall manager shouting 'another win on the tombola' each time a winning ticket is drawn. In fact, Mick is so well known for it that it is quite often shouted out at him down the pub.

Andy Shaw sat me down in a pub one Sunday evening. He'd seen me bring along this tombola stall to the Bedford Beer Festival for a number of years and he suggested that the running of tombola stalls should be rolled out throughout CAMRA as he realised how much they raised.

We put our thinking caps together – who might be interested in coming along to such a meeting? There was about ten of us that met in a pub in Bedford in 1985 and at that meeting we agreed to form the committee.

We'd worked out where to source prizes that seemed to be suitable, which were often items you can get from breweries such as bar towels, ashtrays, beer mats and such like. And you could buy bottles of beer and so on. We were encouraging people to take tombola stalls at their own beer festivals.

MICK SLAUGHTER, CAMRA Fundraising

Once a central collection of breweriana began to form, it made sense for Mick to look at which pub games could be adapted for festivals so that customers could win more prizes.

There is quite a lot of games that you see in pubs where we could come up with a scoring system that gave people a chance to win. And if you give them a chance to win, then they'll spend money trying to get a prize. We must have about 15 or more different pub games that you can now find at beer festivals around the country.

We'd take along some games that are established, such as table skittles or Shut the Box, the dice game. And each time we had a new idea we'd introduce them at different beer festivals to test them. So we came up with an idea of a hoopla game. We used a hand-pump and wooden rings to get round it. So it was just called ring the handpump. We took that up to the Bolton beer festival, myself and a gentleman called Frank Parrington, who was our store man at the time.

As the years have progressed, we've now managed to get a stock of these games in the warehouse at St Albans. We've taken some dying games and made them more widely available, like Toad in the Hole, which was only available in the area around Lewes in East Sussex, or an even rarer one is Caves in Suffolk, a game we've only ever seen in one pub. And we've got a skittles game called Dadlums from Kent. I think that's only available in a couple of pubs as well.

MICK SLAUGHTER, CAMRA Fundraising

CAMRA festivals can source their own prizes and run their own games, or use a central stock. The games are obviously much loved by festival-goers. The Games and Collectables Committee have generated over £50,000 at one GBBF alone. Since 1985, the total raised for the Campaign is close to £1.5m.

THE GREAT BRITISH BEER FESTIVAL

SADLY for CAMRA, Covent Garden wasn't available for another national beer festival in 1976. In the absence of a suitable alternative being found the event took a hiatus for a year and returned in 1977 with a new venue, and a new name. The Great British Beer Festival (GBBF) began in earnest at London's Alexandra Palace.

One interesting nugget that seems to have been lost in the mists of time is that CAMRA were actually invited by Greater London Council to run a Queen's Silver Jubilee beer festival at the same venue in the June of 1977 as well. The *Reading Evening Post* reported that 'there is a mobile zoo, folk groups and steel bands to occupy the bodies and minds of any members of the family for whom beer is not an end unto itself'. But, despite the entertainment, it appears not everyone was impressed by the patriotic ale extravaganza.

On the other side of town, at a middle class jubilee beer festival in Alexandra Park in North London, a young teen in a sleeveless orange tee-shirt reading "Booze" and shoulder-length red curls was less enthusiastic.

Taking a sip of his beer as he listened to the endless medieval songs being played by a local rock band, he told us how "I'm very anti-Jubilee. And I'm very anti-monarchy. There's been nothing but mass hysteria in the last few weeks. People are overreacting to the situation. And the mass hysteria might get worse. Everything is wrong with our country and people just forget about it. They just have a big celebration and forget about everything,"

The Reading Evening Post, 8 June 1977

This two-day event provided the organising committee with a valuable trial run in situ before their first GBBF in the September – the biggest event they'd ever attempted.

The Queen's Silver Jubilee beer festival served 50,000 pints, while the five-day GBBF in September saw 50,000 people drinking 200,000 pints of 144 different real ales from 70 brewers.

GBBF Over the Years

1977 – The First GBBF at Alexandra Palace, London

The Ally Pally might sound like a grand, glamorous home for the festival, but it was in fact rather tatty and run-down at the time, stuck out on a hill-top in the North London suburbs. On the organising committee, we were by no means confident that it would attract the same number of customers as Covent Garden had done, so advance publicity was paramount. It had to be free advance publicity, as well. We had enough money for posters and fliers and so on, but there was nothing in the budget for advertising. As with everything that CAMRA did in those early days, we had to rely on editorial coverage to publicise what we were up to. It helped no end that our cause always seemed to be particularly popular among the journalistic fraternity.

ANTHONY GIBSON, GBBF organising committee;
Extract taken with permission from *Westcountryman: A life in farming, cricket, countryside and cider* (Charlcombe Books, 2021)

Calling it The Great British Beer Festival was something of a masterstroke from the Working Party. It gave the event the sense of scale and importance that it deserved. The first GBBF was opened by Terry Jones of Monty Python (and Penrhos Brewery), who poured pints of beer over his head during the opening while saying, 'beer tasting should be different from wine tasting. You can tell that it's real ale from the way it dribbles down your shoulders.'

He was drying himself and changing his shirt when two photographers from national papers, who really were wearing raincoats and trilbies, came up to him and said: "'Ere Tel, we didn't get that – would you mind doing it again?" To his eternal credit, he then poured two more pints over his head!

ROGER PROTZ, Editor of *The Good Beer Guide*
1978–1984 and 2000–2018

What's Brewing October 1977

Committee member Anthony Gibson added further to the splendour by arranging a parade of horse-drawn brewers' drays. 'They made a magnificent sight as they snorted and stamped along the terrace outside the Palace,' he said.

1978 – Alexandra Palace and the birth of the Champion Beer of Britain

Anthony Gibson was still on board with the festival committee in the run up to the 1978 GBBF, also held at Alexandra Palace. He came up with a novel idea for attracting more publicity.

> The number of breweries was up from 50 to 70 but it struck me midway through the first day that it was all a bit samey. We needed something new and exciting to get us noticed in the national press. It was as I was walking back through the main hall towards the committee room, after having a pee, that the thought struck me. Here we've got hundreds of the best beers in the country all under one roof. Why not organise a competition to find out which are the best, or at least the most popular? And we could call it the "CAMRA Beer of the Year Competition"!
>
> The idea seemed to meet with general approval so I straight-away set to work. A press release was issued, the volunteers manning the bars were asked to nominate their best sellers in each of the various categories. I'd decided that we would do the judging on the following day, using ordinary punters recruited from around the hall. When the time came, I managed to persuade a representative cross-section of ages and sexes to take to the stage and, with me on the PA, away we went. What would eventually become the CAMRA "Champion Beer of Britain" competition, one of the most prestigious events in the British brewing calendar, was off and running. I've always regarded it as one of the more notable feathers in my cap.
>
> ANTHONY GIBSON, GBBF Committee 1978;
> Extract taken with permission from *Westcountryman: A life in farming, cricket, countryside and cider* (Charlcombe Books, 2021)

The jury of 12, selected from drinkers at the festival, tasted the nine top beers and chose their overall winners. Ridley won the bitter category,

Thwaites the mild, and Fuller's Extra Special Bitter was named the best strong ale. The overall Beer of the Year was adjudged to be a dead heat between Thwaites and Fuller's. Despite not winning the top prize, Ridley of Essex were so pleased to take the bitter title that they gave their employees a day's holiday.

For the first few years, finalists were nominated by festival-goers on the day. The award could be, and was, infiltrated by local bias. The shortlist at the 1982 festival in Leeds had a decidedly Northern leaning, although it must be noted that Fuller's still managed to overcome this, taking the top prize for their ESB.

The problem did not go unnoticed by the membership, with one disgruntled punter complaining in *What's Brewing* that the results 'surely reflect the area from which most of the testers originated, rather than the actual quality of the beer'.

Gradually, the awards were overhauled. The competition's name was changed to the Champion Beer of Britain (CBoB) in 1987. By this time, there were six categories being judged; mild bitters, standard bitters, best bitters, special bitters, strong ales and new breweries. To avoid any perceptions of impropriety, the shortlist was voted for by the entire CAMRA membership with independent panels at the festival judging the category winners and a final panel choosing an overall winner.

*   *   *

Today, the process of judging CBoB remains roughly the same. It takes about a year from start to finish. CAMRA members take part in an annual online vote for their favourites and nominations also come from trained CAMRA tasting panels. There are 12 cask beer styles and two strength categories for bottled beers taken into consideration. Area competitions are held at local festivals to assess the nominated beers across nine regions, with the top scorers going on to a final judging in the national competitions: the Champion Beer of Britain, the Champion Winter Beer of Britain (CWBoB) and the Champion Bottled Beer of Britain. 'We've trained hundreds and hundreds now. The beer judging course that we run is specifically aimed at people who judge for CAMRA, but we do get people along who judge for other competitions too.' Christine Cryne, CAMRA Training.

Judging the Champion Beer of Britain competition and the 2023 winners, Elland Brewery

I have been fortunate to judge at both the CBoB and CWBoB national finals, which are usually held at the corresponding GBBF. Six style categories are judged at each festival, with the winners going forward to a final judging panel that names the overall champion. It's always exciting to arrive and discover which category you have been chosen to judge.

I was on the session pales, golden and blond ales at the GBBF 2023 judging and given the honour of selecting the CWBoB at GBBF Winter 2024, where our panel crowned Sarah Hughes Brewery's Snowflake as the victor.

We judge on appearance, aroma, taste and aftertaste. Each category has a certain number of points that can be allocated. The perfect beer would receive a score of 50.

The interesting thing about CAMRA competitions is that 'quaffability' is key: does the appearance and aroma make you want to drink it; do you enjoy the experience of drinking it; and does the aftertaste leave you wanting another one? While this is a very subjective approach, it makes perfect sense for CAMRA as a consumer organisation. They want their Champion to be the most drinkable for the widest spectrum of people. If you don't like, or don't normally drink, a particular style, you are encouraged to judge as if you were making a recommendation for a friend, so the beer scores fairly for its quality and isn't marked down because it doesn't happen to be to your taste.

The expertise and variety of backgrounds of the people around the judging table also helps to stop personal bias from creeping in. Over the years I've judged with fellow beer writers – many of whom have judged beer competitions around the world – publicans, brewers, industry leaders and no shortage of CAMRA members who have undergone Tasting Panel training and have plenty of years of experience under their belts. This leads to some lively debate during the sessions, although there is no need for the panel to reach a consensus. Our scores are tallied separately and the winner is the top scorer.

The judging session traditionally starts with a jug of a non-competition beer being brought round and judges being served a small glass. This palate livener is taken usually at around 9am before an intense couple of hours of beer scrutiny. I suspect that Christine Cryne, chair of the national judging panel, chooses something that she rates particularly highly from the festival. Often it is a traditional bitter.

All of the nominated beers are judged blind, and good form
dictates that you don't even try to guess what the beer is – just judge
what is in your glass on its own merits. This is a far cry from Roger
Protz's experience in 1980, judging the final live on stage with fellow
beer writer Michael Jackson. He was booed when the crowd realised
that 'Londoner born and boozed could not pick out Young's tasty brew'.
Failing to identify Young's bitter, of which he had 'sunk more than a
few gallons' in his time, was an unforgivable transgression.

Roger seems to have made winding up festival goers a bit of a habit:

> In 2004, it was my fate to be booed at GBBF when I announced
> Greene King IPA had won a silver award in CBoB. Don't shoot
> the messenger. I also appeared on TV with Michael Jackson
> and we were asked to judge a beer blind and say what it was.
> MJ cleverly dodged the question but I stupidly said I thought it
> was Tim Taylor's Landlord. Turned out to be John Smith's bitter.
> I'm surprised I still have a reputation.
>
> ROGER PROTZ, Champion Beer Writer

The judging room falls quiet as the first tasting is delivered.
Pocket torches are used to inspect the colour and clarity of dark beers.
Glasses are swirled and aromas inhaled. Each beer is judged in silent
solitude before the table comes back to discuss their thoughts. Luckily
there are always two score sheets in front of you – one for scribbling
as you go and one for best. This means that you can always go back
to rescore if necessary: often you can go in too high or too low on the
initial samples and need to recalibrate.

Sitting on the panel to judge the overall champion is surely the
most difficult job. You feel the pressure behind every sip you take,
knowing what is riding on your decision. Additionally, you are trying
to identify 'The Best' from a range of styles that may not be directly
comparable. Happily, the CAMRA judging criteria are on hand to
support you in formulating a score. While no system is perfect, this
one is pretty robust.

Only once the final champion has been selected can the judges
hope to discover the names of the beers they judged. This is helpful,
not just to help you decide what you are going to drink at the beer
festival once it opens, but also to flag the hidden prejudices you may

have been harbouring against particular styles or beers. There is always some surprise – a beer that you thought you loved which you marked low, or vice versa. Judging is a humbling experience!

At the 2023 GBBF I was judging Champion Beer of Britain alongside journalist John Porter: 'There's no cost to enter, the local CAMRA branches put their favourite beers through. So in that sense, it's Darwinism in action. It is the beers that people really enjoy that come through the competition. And it's important because the beers that win it are iconic. I'm thinking of beers like Timothy Taylor's Landlord. Or Surrey Hills Shere Drop. They become part of the national landscape. And for the brewers it can be a massive cash injection because people will actively go out and seek a Champion beer.' (John Porter, journalist and beer sommelier.)

The CAMRA membership, and the public at large, doesn't always agree with the final results. The victory of Ind Coope's Burton Ale in 1990 raised more than a few eyebrows, since their parent company, Allied, was one of the notorious Big Six breweries that CAMRA had been campaigning against for 20 years. Writing a letter to *What's Brewing* to express his concerns, Surrey/Hants Borders Branch member Bob Southwell expressed his alarm at the choice of Champion: 'My worst fear is for the "new" drinker to be encouraged by the "Champion" award only to be given an expensive disappointment... As an organisation we stand to be brought into a certain amount of disrepute.' (*What's Brewing*, September 1990.)

The furore over Greene King's Abbot Ale coming second place in the 2023 competition was so intense that it completely overshadowed the achievement of the ultimate winner, Elland Brewery, in the media. 'Angry real ale fans all frothed up amid claims champion beer contest was rigged,' hyperventilated *The Sun*.

For me, the talk of rigged competitions and unworthy winners smacks of some rather unpleasant gatekeeping in the cask ale world. Abbot Ale was the sixth biggest selling cask ale brand in the UK in 2023. Some CAMRA members must be buying it – and often enjoying it.

Everyone is entitled to have their own preferences. I've had my fair share of poorly kept Greene King ales in their tied pubs, so I am under no illusions that their quality can be ... questionable. And one can certainly find fault in the way that macro brewers maintain a stranglehold on pubs, which limits independent brewers' routes to market. But to suggest that some beers are 'acceptable' champions whilst others are not is just plain snobbery. They all jump the same hurdles to get through the competition and the best on the day will win.

Lifting the CBoB trophy has classically led to a significant uplift in sales. Fuller's reported a 25% increase in demand for Chiswick Bitter in the immediate aftermath of its 1989 win. George Bateman was enthusiastic when interviewed about his brewery's win with XXXB in 1986, saying the honour was worth more than anything the brewing professionals could bestow: 'It was voted upon and judged by the people who really count – the beer drinkers themselves. It's one of the finest honours I have ever known and it's given us a real boost to consolidate and expand our outlets.' (George Bateman speaking to the *Lincolnshire Standard and Boston Guardian*, Thursday, 28 August 1986)

Champions with their beer JHB in 2001, Oakham Ales had to start brewing six times a week rather than three after their success. The win was ultimately the catalyst for Oakham Ales' move from their 35-barrel plant at the Brewery Tap in central Peterborough to their current 75-barrel brewery in Woodston, providing the final push for them to take the leap and invest in expansion.

In 2019 Surrey Hills Brewery took the last gong before the COVID-19 pandemic stopped play for three years. Founder Ross Hunter reported a 'massive demand' for Shere Drop after it was named Champion.

> Wholesalers and pub companies, as well as independent free-houses, were all trying to get hold of the beer. Our focus was on keeping our loyal existing customers satisfied and then prioritising new orders. We also worked hard to ensure that our other beers all continued to be brewed. We were keen for nothing to change at the brewery as a result of the win, although of course, the awareness of the brewery across the country increased.
>
> We have been in the final stages of judging almost every year since the brewery started back in 2005 and I thought our big moment was when Hammer Mild won Mild Gold and Bronze in the Overall Champion in 2010. To win CBoB in 2019 felt unreal, particularly when you look at the illustrious list of predecessors.
>
> ROSS HUNTER, Founder of Surrey Hills Brewery

The most decorated cask ale is Timothy Taylor's Landlord, which has won the Punters' Prize, as it was described by *The Mirror*, four times. The Queen of Pop herself, Madonna, said that she developed a taste for Landlord at the Dog and Duck in Soho on Jonathan Ross's BBC talk show in 2003, then called it the 'Champagne of ales' on Michael Parkinson's ITV talk show in 2005.

It would appear that Madge is also partial to visiting the odd beer festival from time to time. 'I'd been approached one year by an agent hiring out celebrity appearances at events. I explained that CAMRA had no funds for such promotions. After the festival I thought I should let him know that Madonna had visited the festival as a paying customer. A handful of people had recognised her on the door; I hadn't.' (Geoff Strawbridge, former CAMRA Regional Director for Greater London.)

Sadly, even CBoB cannot work miracles. Winning the prestigious accolade for the second time in August 2023, fans rightly toasted the success of the 1872 Porter from Elland Brewery. However, just six months later, the company entered liquidation. This is a cautionary tale about the difficulties British brewers are facing at the moment when costs are spiralling and consumer spending is down.

It was a privilege to judge the Champion Beer of Britain's final round in 2024, at the Kelham Hall Beer Festival. Despite an extremely tight competition, my fellow judges and I found Crouch Vale's Amarillo to be the winner. Crouch Vale are no strangers to this success – their Brewers Gold did the double, winning CBoB in 2005 and 2006.

Perhaps mindful of the fate of Elland Brewery, and certainly well accustomed to the vagaries of the industry by decades of experience, co-founder and brewer Colin Bocking was cautious in reflecting on Crouch Vale's success when I spoke to him a couple of weeks after the victory:

> It's great to get the award and get some industry recognition of what we are doing. There's been a number of new enquiries and quite a bit of extra interest as a result of the award and that can only be good for trade. However, I fear that cask ale has a rather old-fashioned and dated image and volumes generally are declining. That is a worry for brewers like us whose main business is cask ale. You only have to go to any beer festival to see it – the attendees are predominantly older, and sadly, with every year which passes,

there are fewer of them. There are exceptions of course, but the youngsters of today don't seem to drink cask beer like we used to when we were young. I don't have a solution, but we have a unique cask beer culture in this country and when well-brewed and served, the product is unsurpassed. We should be shouting it from the rooftops!

COLIN BOCKING, Crouch Vale Brewery

1979 – Alexandra Palace, London

The third edition of GBBF was opened by TV botanist and noted beer lover David Bellamy. Given the tagline 'the beer festival that's something else', it certainly boasted a lot of added extras. There was a firework display, a rally of historic vehicles and a parade of horse-drawn drays. Not forgetting the special jazz concert given by the Ronnie Scott Quartet.

The event was confirmed as one of truly national significance by a special agreement made with British Rail giving people across the UK up to a 50% discount on a return fare to Wood Green during the festival period. Under the scheme, a return fare from Edinburgh cost the princely sum of £19.65.

One of the most significant additions was a German evening on the Wednesday night, which not only involved the post-apocalyptic noisescape of a traditional Oompah band, but also saw European beers coming to GBBF for the first time.

The Great Fire of Alexandra Palace: 30 August–6 September 1980

I was down with family on my father's side in London. And I was a bit of a punk in those days. So I was on the tube train, going up to Kings Road, just to see what was going on. I spotted a fly poster in the tube for a beer festival at Alexandra Palace. I thought, that looks like more fun than shopping. So I got onto the relevant tube, got to Alexandra Palace and wandered into this tent – because that was the year that Alexander Palace burned down. I found lots and lots of people and all these barrels and wooden things and taps. And I thought, this looks good, I'm enjoying this.

DENNY CORNELL-HOWARTH, 37 years of GBBF volunteering

The Alexandra Palace in North London inconveniently decided to burn down on Thursday, 10th June 1980, less than three months before GBBF was booked to take place. In fairness, the landmark had survived better than its original incarnation, which has completely burnt out once before, 14 days after it first opened in June 1873.

Festival organisers raced to find an alternative venue. There were intense negotiations with Haringey Council about their legal liability to provide a suitable space. CAMRA stood to lose out, not only on the expected profit but also their upfront outlay.

In the end, by agreement, the festival was hosted in two giant marquees just down the hill on the old racecourse at Alexandra Park. It was officially opened by illustrator Bill Tidy, who produced the much-loved Kegbuster cartoon for CAMRA's *What's Brewing* magazine for 42 years. A crew of over 500 volunteers served 200,000 pints to some 80,000 thirsty guests.

The Great Hall at Alexandra Palace after the fire, looking towards the main stage — where the pub games were held last year.
Picture: John Cogill

What's Brewing, August 1980

'I would like to give special thanks for all the helpers who worked hard under what at times were pretty appalling conditions,' organiser Pat O'Neill said to *What's Brewing*. 'What with melting ice and the occasional rain shower, it got pretty muddy behind the bars.'

They got through ten tons of ice, as well as hiring three refrigerated trailers from Trumans to keep the beer in good condition. But Pat still thought the beer was drinking better than it had at any of the three previous festivals. The mud was no joke though. In reality, the heavy rain could have scuppered the whole event.

We arrived on site and the marquees were fine, the security fence was good and workable, and we set about building the stillage out of the usual scaffolding. Thank God that those of us who had run beer festivals outdoors said to put scaffold planks under the scaffold feet to help distribute the weight.

About a day after we opened, it started raining, and the ground got wetter and wetter, and I noticed that the poles for the marquees and the beer stillage, etc. were all starting to sink into the ground. More alarmingly, after about day four, I noticed that when I walked round the site, it was like walking on a rather soggy trampoline – the ground slowly bounced in a wave-like motion as you trod over it (and in my defence, your honour, I was still only about 10 stone then). I looked around and realised that Haringey had given us a site on top of a filled-in Victorian sewage station and the pancake layer on the top was about to cave in! I had a vision, fortunately not realised, of the whole thing sinking through the floor and taking with it all the beer, 25,000 fairly heavy customers and the whole of CAMRA's leadership and most active volunteers – literally totally in the shit! In the end the worst thing was having to dig out everything that had sunk around 50cm into the ground, and that was nearly everything that had any weight on it.

TONY MILLNS, GBBF Working Party

Tony thinks that having a 'come what may' attitude to the festival after Ally Pally burned down was the wrong decision in hindsight: 'There was an absolutely apocalyptic photo of the blaze, with flames leaping about the height of the main tower, taking up most of the front page of the *Evening Standard,* footage on TV news and photos the following day. Every reasonable person in London must have concluded the GBBF would be cancelled. Attendance was relatively low and though we didn't make a loss, I don't think we made much of a profit.' (Tony Millns, GBBF Working Party.)

1981 – Queen's Hall, Leeds

With the Alexandra Palace out of action, and the Campaign for Real Ale's 10th anniversary looming, the decision was made to take the GBBF out of London for the first time in 1981. It was moved to Leeds, the start of a decade of the festival trundling slowly around the country before settling back in the capital from 1991.

It was a big deal, as back in those days we were used to drinking a limited range of beers dictated to us by the tied houses in the area where we lived. Leeds at that time was dominated by Tetleys, and excellent that so much of it was in those days, the opportunity to sample a wide variety of beers from all over the country – ironically in a location only a few hundred yards from the Tetley's brewery – was one not to be missed. Talk about kids in a sweetshop…
The old former tram shed, with its huge floorspace and cavernous interior, made an excellent location for the festival, and the bigwigs at CAMRA HQ must have thought so too; the festival returned again the following year.

CHRIS DYSON, writing in *Real Ale, Real Music* in 2021

The festival benefitted from the support and ingenuity of the local branch, who found a novel way to promote the event:

I look at the size of the marketing department within CAMRA for GBBF now and I think back to that first Great British Beer Festival in Leeds. There were six of us in the local branch, sat in the Packhorse pub up on Woodhouse Moor. Somebody said, we need to put some posters around Leeds for GBBF.

I went, I don't mind doing that. I've got me motorcycle. In those days I rode a 650 Suzuki motorcycle and it had two very useful panniers. For those people that don't really know motorcycle things, if you think of an old fashioned toilet cistern with a liftoff lid … They had solid bottoms and were waterproof. I filled one of the panniers with wallpaper paste and the other pannier with rolled up posters.

Me and the then boyfriend drove around Leeds in the dead of night, fly-posting everywhere. Probably desperately looked down upon now. I think we did somewhere in the region of 800 posters. So it was quite a bit of work. I think my proudest one was in the centre of Leeds. There is a very nice statue because Leeds is twinned with Dortmund. A lovely statue of a man with a great big beer barrel. And I posted a poster right on the front of his beer barrel. I was quite pleased with that.

DENNY CORNELL-HOWARTH, Desecrater (or Decorator) of The Dortmund Drayman

The move up North couldn't have come at a better time for CAMRA. After 10 years of often thankless campaigning, the first national festival in Leeds seems to have invigorated a lot of members. While the 1981 GBBF was a slow starter – and only two-thirds of the beer ordered was eventually drunk – Leeds proved fertile ground for the Campaign, with 300 new members signed up and thousands more newly educated about cask ale. 'It was obvious that, unlike the position in London, many drinkers were being introduced to real ales from other parts of the UK for the first time. In an area still dominated by Webster and Tetley tied houses, with club keg beer and John Smiths maintaining a strong influence, the GBBF came as an enlightenment and positive education to many.' (Robert Walker writing to the *What's Brewing* letters page in October 1981.)

The campaigning vibe was strong, with customers flocking to fill in a form urging John Smiths to return to brewing cask ale. Feelings were high, and no small amount of scorn was poured on the brewer, not least an intriguing reference in *What's Brewing* to a John Smiths-related sign which somehow found its way above the toilet door.

*   *   *

The first GBBF in Leeds was also a pivotal moment in the development of beer festivals globally. It was visited by one Charlie Papazian, the founder of the American Homebrewers Association and the Brewers Association.

My primary contact was [beer writer] Michael Jackson, who I had met earlier that year. He came to the Home Brewers Conference in June. He was extraordinarily supportive of what we were doing. He invited me personally to come by and have a pint at his local.

I hung out with him and stayed with him in Hammersmith in London and explored the pub scene. Eventually, we both went to Leeds. I'll never forget that first impression I had when I walked into the hall and I saw all these people and all these different kinds of beers and ales.

When I walked into the hall and saw the beer culture everywhere, this awareness of beer and how it was made, how it was to be served, we had none of it. We didn't have any of that in the United States. I wondered if we could ever have something called the Great American Beer Festival in the United States.

I proposed that idea to Michael. He said, that would be a great idea, Charlie, but where are you going to get the beer? He was right. You know, the beers in the United States, what were you going to get? Light lager. You couldn't really have a quality beer festival by just serving light lager. But we figured out a way to make it work. I came back and proposed the idea to some friends, and everybody thought we were crazy. But that's when you know you have a good idea, when people think you're crazy. So we tried to figure out how we could make the Great American Beer Festival truly great and develop and nurture a culture of beer appreciation in the United States.

The experience, enthusiasm and the passion that CAMRA had was really what I respected. That whole idea of celebrating a beer culture was fantastic. And I admire them so much for being able to pull off the events in those early times and continuing to this day.

CHARLIE PAPAZIAN, Founder of the
Great American Beer Festival (GABF)

Charlie wasted no time in getting to work. The first GABF was presented by the Brewers Association and took place in Boulder, Colorado, in June 1982. It featured 47 beers from 24 breweries. The festival moved to Denver in 1984, which has been its home ever since. It is now one of the most important beer festivals in the world, with more than 500 breweries showcasing over 2.000 beers to 40,000 guests.

We purposefully avoided having any ubiquitous mass produced light lagers at our festival. There wasn't any information about what people were making except the beer bottle collectors and the beer label collectors and the can collectors had books of labels. That's what we used to figure out what some of the regional breweries were making in the United States.

We did find people that were making porters and ales, and German-style beers that were specialty beers and usually only regionally available. Things that you just never would know about unless you lived in that area of the brewery. These breweries were going out of business left and right. So those were the beers that we invited. The breweries agreed to donate the beer on the premise that we were going to be celebrating American beer culture – what we had in the past and what we foresaw for the future.

There was a gentleman named Fred Huber. His family had a brewery in Wisconsin for over a hundred years and he was the current president and CEO. He had come to our event to see what he was donating his beer to. He was an older gentleman with a lot of beer experience. He was sitting at the table and he saw all these people, mostly younger people, trying all these different beers from all these different breweries under one roof. He was stunned. He said, "I never thought I would ever live to see a day like this."

What he was observing was the very first time different breweries were serving their beer at one event. Usually a beer festival before the Great American Beer Festival was one brand and people drinking a lot of it and not understanding one thing about what they were drinking. And here he saw all these people not only enjoying the diversity of beer but they were talking about the beer. Everybody was talking about where the beer came from, who made it, how it was made. That was just a novel, unique and revolutionary notion in those days.

CHARLIE PAPAZIAN, Founder of the
Great American Beer Festival (GABF)

1983 – Bingley Hall, Birmingham

After two years in Leeds, GBBF hit the Midlands. It was the second festival organised by National Executive member (and coincidentally Birmingham born) Tim Webb. After signing the hire contract for Bingley Hall, the Working Party discovered that the venue was some-what lacking in toilet facilities. As CAMRA is a broad church, they fortunately had one of the regional staff of Portaloo amongst their membership. He negotiated with the company to provide the first ever multi-storey Portaloo facility as a temporary urinal.

The queue lengthens as thirsty drinkers wait for the opening of the Great British Beer Festival in Birmingham last month. To find out what happened inside, see P 6-7.

What's Brewing October 1983

The publicity team for the festival included many local journalists, and even the original producer of the soap Emmerdale. They were able to procure the Warwickshire and England cricket captain Bob Willis to open the festival. The County Championship match at Edgbaston – Warwickshire versus Glamorgan – was rained off on the second day, and so most of the players turned up to the festival. When the weather cleared overnight, Warwickshire pulled off one of the most impressive fourth innings victories in Championship history, helped by a blistering 243 not out by West Indian international Alvin Kallicharan, who had chosen not to attend GBBF the night before. 'Given the number of fielders, strike bowlers and opening batsmen who had to be carried into taxis at the end of the evening, I found the victory not that difficult to explain.' (Tim Webb, festival organiser.)

The festival was also notable for featuring the first female GBBF bar manager, Sarah Edmonson. Tim sees the festival as a turning point for beer in Birmingham. During the 1970s the pubs were almost entirely owned by Ansells or Bass Charrington, with 12 under the local independent Davenports and the last seven or so appearing to be freehouses but in reality actually being tied to the larger brewers. After 1983 the city began to open up to other breweries, largely, Tim suggests, down to the impact of such a successful event.

'The police brought a panda car on site, the festival was so huge. There was a hog roast on the go and while the police were walking off in one direction, someone got the head off the hog roast and put it on their car. They weren't best amused.' (Mark Parkes, West Midlands Regional Deputy Director.)

Meanwhile, the German organisers of a Bavarian-style beer festival due to be held over 10 days at Villa Park in the same year was cancelled with just two weeks to go, after questions from environmental health about food preparation, sanitary arrangements and noise, with the police also expressing reservations about granting a drinks licence. They clearly didn't have the same organisational pedigree as CAMRA.

1985 – Metropole, Brighton

Under the leadership of festival organiser John Cryne, GBBF was moved to the Brighton Metropole for its 1985 iteration. It was hoped that the event would prove popular with seaside tourists after the 1984 festival had been cancelled due to Birmingham's Bingley Hall burning down (an all-too-frequent occurrence in the early years of GBBF!) An alternative 'Not the Great British Beer Festival' had been run at Digbeth Civic Hall in Birmingham in September 1984 to make up for the cancellation.

The folding of boxes for festival glasses at Brighton 1990

The new Brighton venue was hailed as a success, with 85,000 pints consumed by 23,000 visitors over five days. This may have been thanks to prices being on average some ten pence cheaper than in the local pubs. This angered local publicans who blamed their tie with the big brewers for the cost of their beer.

CAMRA didn't miss a beat in capitalising on this campaigning opportunity. They highlighted the threat to choice posed by brewer takeovers, laying wreaths in memory of ales once brewed by Yates & Jackson and Simpkiss on the stillage. Visitors were also invited to sign a pledge in protest at the Scottish & Newcastle's takeover bid for Matthew Brown.

The festival was the first to feature a family room, with magicians and Punch and Judy shows stages throughout the festival to keep the kids entertained.

A crew of 350 CAMRA volunteers ran the festival – including Phil Child from Elgin. It was his third GBBF, and he had driven 45 miles to Inverness, then flown to Gatwick before taking the train to Brighton to do his stint on the bar.

*   *   *

The first Brighton GBBF saw the birth of Bières Sans Frontières (BSF) as the first dedicated Continental beer stand was presented to an eager public. It housed a range of mostly bottle-conditioned beers from Germany, Belgium and Czechoslovakia, as it then was. Allegedly, it took nearly two hours to deposit the empties in the local bottle bank!

The introduction of an international bar was a bitter pill for some CAMRA members to swallow, however.

> I deplore the selling of foreign beers at beer festivals – these are irrelevant to CAMRA's main aim of generating interest in traditional cask beers. I used to take great delight, when serving at beer festivals in replying to "Got any lager mate?" with "No, sir. This is a beer festival – the nearest thing we've got is lemonade!" Now I have to point them in the direction of the Grölsch.
>
> JEFF TUCKER – Grumpy of Snodland, Kent writing to the letters page of *What's Brewing* in November 1985

BSF is a particular strength of the GBBF, providing easy access to beers from around the world which are often hard, if not impossible, to source privately in the UK. Such is the demand that it now occupies four bars and includes casks, kegs, bottles and cans.

Rumour has it that a secret party arranges an exchange of a shipping container of beer with the Great American Beer Festival each year, ensuring an unmatched selection of hard-to-find American beers. Many of the visitors to GBBF 2023 that I interviewed cited the American cask bars as one of the key reasons for their attendance.

Pete Harkins of Backbeat Brewing Co of Beverly, MA

Right from the offset it was evident that the American beers were a big attraction and this was all down to the efforts of one person. Johnathan Tuttle was listed in *What's Brewing* as the North American contact for CAMRA, he helped found NERAX (New England Real Ale Exhibition) and had been a frequent visitor to the UK. He personally sourced all the American beers, both bottle and cask, using his skills as a Trade Union Organiser and ordained priest to persuade American brewers to donate beer to GBBF. The American bar was a magnet for aspiring "craft" brewers as we had rarely seen American beers on sale.

German beers were courtesy of Olaf Schellenberg who was a one-man import business driving a seven-tonne Mercedes van around Bavarian breweries and bringing them over to the UK. It's interesting to note that a current 'on trend' German beer is Tegernseer, something we had been selling since the early 90s. Belgian and Dutch beers came courtesy of Hugh Shipman and Marlies Boink, and their exacting standards meant we were getting only the best.

We have regularly had rapidly selling beers as word seems to spread. Coopers Sparkling Ale was a big seller in the 90s as hordes of Aussies descended on the bar. One year Boston Lager sold so quickly that I had to ask Shepherd Neame (the importers) if they could sell us some extra (they had donated 20 cases). Another year it was Lion Stout from Sri Lanka, which we had to get extra in after the first day.

Expansion was gradual, and, thankfully, encouraged as the bars were highly profitable. Expansion brought problems with having to increase supply but we were able to debut many beers, Little Creatures and Stone & Wood from Australia, Bernard from Czechia, Lervig from Norway, and, of course, the fantastic Italian beers promoted by Kuaska. Expanding the USA range of cask fell to new American volunteers and the bottles and cans became the responsibility of the Brewers Association Export Development Program.

In 1998, we held our first overseas "planning" meeting at Bier Circus in Brussels, since then we have held our annual meetings in Germany, Czechia, The Netherlands, Spain, Belgium and Italy – always including at least one brewery visit.

IAN GARRETT, BSF since 1994

1990 – Brighton, Metropole

The festival was characterised by a venue Catering Manager who was paranoid about having their licence taken away, despite us having proven that we could run a successful and trouble-free event at the same venue, Brighton Metropole, from 1985 to 1987. As a result we had many strange restrictions placed on us, including having one of their bar staff on each of our bars to "supervise" and in the end doing very little other than getting in the way. Also, at the insistence of the local police, every souvenir glass that was taken off site had to be in a cardboard box. The staff bar session once the festival had closed was thus mainly spent by everyone making up the flatpacked boxes ready to be used the next day.

JOHN NORMAN, GBBF festival organiser

1991 – London, Docklands

London Docklands was far more successful than we had anticipated. The venue was in financial difficulty, so when we arrived on site we were informed that the desk phones only worked for incoming calls. They gave us a small number of early "brick" type mobile phones to use for outgoing calls.

The air conditioning that we had hoped would cool the beer also was not functioning as expected, but that was less of an issue as the beer was being sold very quickly. So much so that a lot of time was spent using the mobile phones to ring round all beer suppliers in the southeast to see what they could let us have.

One larger supplier in West London had the beer but nobody to drive the truck once loaded. Fortunately, we had someone who could drive such a vehicle and it was agreed that he could be sent over by train to collect the loaded vehicle. This ended up happening several times over the weekend so that in the end the majority of the company's fleet was parked outside the exhibition hall.

On Monday morning they sent their drivers over to collect the vehicles which by then had been loaded with all the empties. I seemed to spend quite a lot of time rolling barrels around that festival.

In the evenings a different problem had to be overcome in that in those days the Dockland Light Railway ceased service mid-evening to be replaced by a bus service. Our customers would have overwhelmed the DLR replacement bus service so we laid on our own, which people then had to be directed towards. The queue for the DLR's replacement bus service still grew quite large, however, and had to be managed by our volunteer staff under threat of the service being suspended.

JOHN NORMAN, GBBF festival organiser

1992 – Olympia, London

In 1992 GBBF began what would be more than a three-decade long love affair with London's Olympia. Christine Cryne made history as the first female festival organiser, the first of four to date. Women have overseen the organisation of roughly a third of all GBBFs.

I'll never forget the buzz I got the first time I opened the Great British Beer Festival in 1992. I've never had such a feeling. It was quite interesting being the first female to run it because you got asked all sorts of dark questions. The usual one was "Do you drink pints?", and "How many pints do you have to drink to get drunk?"

But it depends on what type of journalist you're talking to. I've done interviews with things like BBC Breakfast News where you would never dream of hearing that to something like *The Sun* or *The Mirror* which will only ask you those sorts of questions.

CHRISTINE CRYNE, GBBF festival organiser

2002 – Olympia, London

I was walking down the side of the Grand Hall, towards the main entrance on the left-hand side. I hear this cheer go up. Usually that means someone's broken a glass. But then the roar moves. I can hear the cheer coming towards me.

When the roar moves, you know there's a streaker. I saw this lad running towards me, stark naked. He was avoiding the stewards because you could see them in their orange t-shirts. But I'm just stood there casually dressed, and he's coming towards me. And I thought, right, how can I grab him?

He'd obviously gone into the toilets, got undressed, put everything in his backpack, and put his backpack on. When he comes running past me, I reached out and I grabbed his backpack and ripped it off his shoulders. He stopped because he realised that I'd got his clothes, his keys, his wallet. Everything. He just stopped and looked at me.

"You! Follow me. NOW" I said. I walked as slowly as I could up to K Gate. He followed me all the way into the yard. And as you go out into the yard, there's a big barrier across the entrance. And on the other side of the road is the pub.

I stood there with his bag. I got him a few feet behind me. A few stewards had come behind him. I said to the Olympia guard on the gate:

"Open the gate, I want him out now."

"No," said the guard. "I can't let him out like that."

So I threw the bag over the road. It landed on the pavement outside the pub. It's his problem now I thought and I walked off. The guard had to let him out and the streaker had to walk across the road naked to the pub. Where there were lots of people sat outside all having a bloody good laugh.

MARC HOLMES, 2002 GBBF Organiser

2004 – The Great Flood of Olympia, London

In 2004 Olympia was struck by a storm of biblical proportions. Lightning struck overhead, followed by a monumental clap of thunder – just after Greene King IPA had been announced as winning gold in the bitter class of the Champion Beer of Britain competition. The downpour that followed overflowed the guttering, causing parts of the venue to flood.

Some chose to interpret the storm as the wrath of God – and the downpour of letters that the Greene King win brought to the *What's Brewing* postbag was allegedly the most correspondence received on a single issue in the publication's history.

The Olympia management team were amazed we stayed open. They said any other show would have closed down due to the amount of water coming in. But I told them that as long as the lights stayed on we would stay open. The thought of throwing everybody out in the torrential rain didn't appeal. All the power had gone to the bars so the cooling had gone off, but of course we were a cash society back then so no card readers.

MARC HOLMES, 2004 GBBF Organiser

A song was penned following the flood: "There's a hole in my festival, dear Goliath, dear Goliath." Goliath was Marc Holmes' call sign on the radios.

I've never come across any situation like it. It's when we found out how leaky the building was, there was literally water pouring through the roof here, there and everywhere. Certain parts of the floor were flooded. I saw a picture in the paper, it was of a van parked at Hammersmith just a mile away. The water was nearly up to the wing mirror. It was a flash flood. The volunteers had to close one bar, but only one. The decision was taken not to put the customers out into the street because it was raining so heavily – it was actually safer to keep them in the building. That shows the professionalism of the volunteers here, how we can pull together in a panic.

DAIGY, Bar Manager of the GBBF's Volunteer Arms

2006 – Earl's Court, London

The first outing at Earl's Court was praised by veteran beer writer Pete Brown for the introduction of third of a pint glasses to allow people to sample more of the range of beers, along with a visual tasting system to help people choose the styles of beer they preferred.

However, Pete was certainly not impressed by the Wychwood Brewery-sponsored volunteer t-shirts, which played on their marketing campaign with the Hobgoblin character saying 'Definitely not for lager boys'. Quite rightly, he criticised the short-sightedness of this approach when looking to entice lager drinkers to try real ale. 'As someone who drinks lager, I felt personally insulted. Someone may try to argue that it should be taken as a joke. All I can say is that if I'm a potential new recruit to the cause who is nervous about what to try, I may not get the humour.' (Pete Brown writing on petebrown.net in 2006.)

Earl's Court, August 2007

2017 – Olympia, London

The great beer sages of our time, Boak and Bailey, wrote on their blog that GBBF 'doesn't quite seem to click in these days'. They blamed competition from other festivals that meant GBBF was no longer the only game in town, as well as the venue being too 'draughty, overwhelming, tiring to schlep around, and dim'.

This is just one example of the criticism that has floated around GBBF in modern times, perhaps more so in the late 2010s before keg beer was finally introduced to the festival. There was a sense, certainly amongst beer writers, that CAMRA's flagship event had lost touch, was too staid, and would eventually fizzle out of existence.

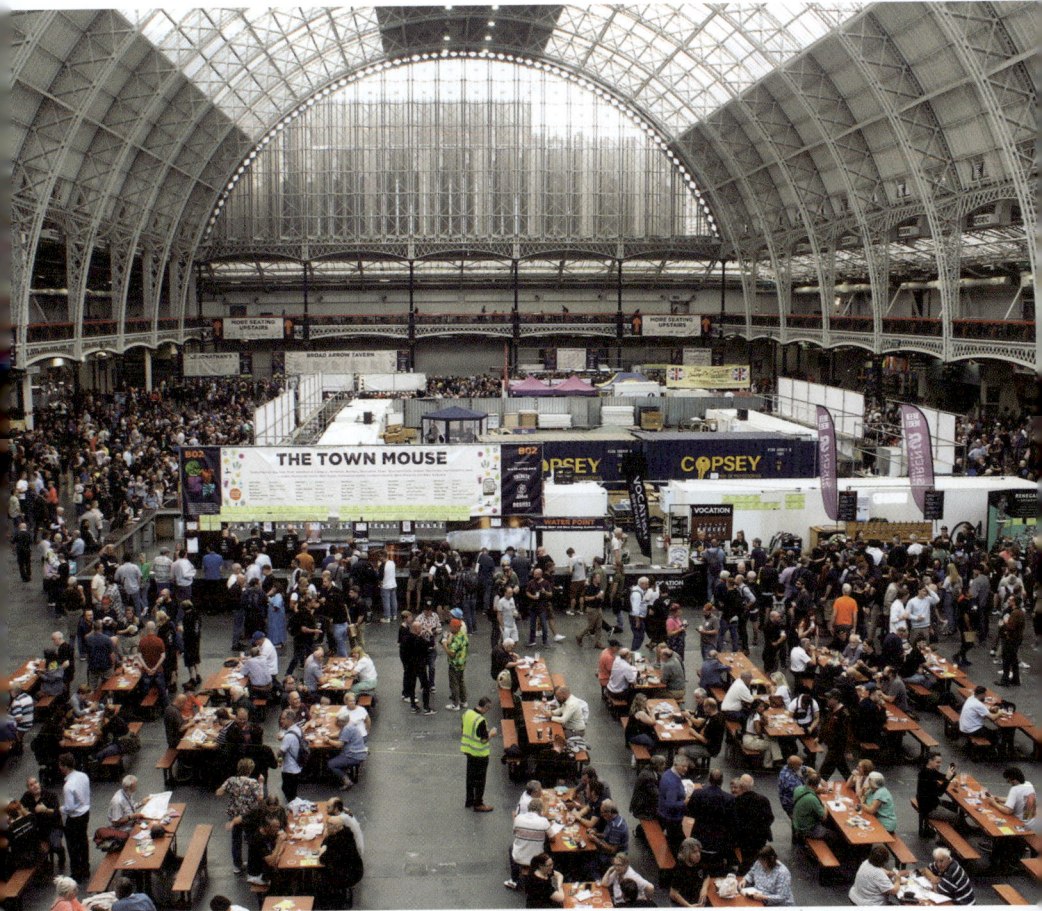

A view over GBBF at Olympia

2023 – Olympia, London

The first serving prime minister to visit GBBF was Rishi Sunak who went on a walkabout at the Tuesday Trade Session in 2023. Teetotaller Sunak was roundly heckled by the crowd and CAMRA was criticised for inviting him by much of the membership, but it was actually something of a masterstroke by the CAMRA marketing team. They fully capitalised on the media attention the visit generated by sending out a press release the next day stating that only 9% of people had faith that the prime minister would look after the interests of pubs.

Cancellation in 2024

In the January, it was announced that GBBF 2024 would be cancelled. Olympia wasn't available on the dates required and ceaseless years of building works at the site were starting to impact on quality. It wasn't possible to find an alternative venue that could host this behemoth of an event in time and the organising committee had simply reached the point of no return.

> I was heartbroken to once again have to cancel GBBF for 2024, having already cancelled it twice during COVID. Olympia was unable to offer us dates in August, which made running the festival almost impossible. We wouldn't have access to the staff accommodation since we use student halls and people were less likely to be able to get the time off work. We will be back in 2025, in a new venue, Birmingham's NEC. It has been strange not having the date fast approaching this year, but as I have handed over the reins to a new organiser, Adam Gent, I will have to get used to it. Though I will obviously still volunteer just in other roles.
>
> CATHERINE TONRY, GBBF festival organiser 2018–2024

The absence of GBBF was a mild inconvenience to regular customers and the breweries who showcase there, but it caused the team of volunteers genuine personal sadness. I spoke to Kath Lilley the week after the festival had been due to take place. 'It's like a long-lost family coming together each year. That's why it's so sad there's no festival this year. The stewards had a get together at the weekend, where they just went and camped so they could all be together and share that bond.

The Bières Sans Frontières team too, a lot of them have gone over to Belgium for a weekend, just for that camaraderie. It's such a big part of so many people's lives.' (Kath Lilley, GBBF volunteer since 1990.)

The 2025 festival in the Midlands will see GBBF head out of London once more for the first time since 1990. It represents a real opportunity for CAMRA to build on 50 years of successful national events and take on the criticism that such a prominent festival can sometimes attract. It will be fascinating to see how the Great British Beer Festival translates into a new venue, a new city, and looks forward to a new future.

The new festival organiser is Adam Gent, who says he was thrust into the role by the former organiser Catherine Tonry. At the time, she told him not to worry because it's not too much work. But then they had to leave Olympia and spend a year hunting for venues, so it was actually rather a lot of work.

Adam Gent

Adam is a safe pair of hands though. He's been involved with the back room operations of GBBF for over a decade, and has been working at beer festivals since he was 18 when he volunteered at the Cardiff festival.

The intention isn't that we go back to a roaming year on year move because we just can't do that anymore. The goal is to try and move it out of London and grow it back up. In the latter stage we got about 25,000 at Olympia. Finger in the air, we can probably get about 30,000 people over the week at the NEC.

In the future, there's more halls we could take, to grow into a larger vessel. At Olympia we were very much landlocked. Hopefully moving into the Midlands gives us a new attendee base and a new volunteer base.

It won't be radically different, at least not to start with. It will still be focused on British beer, but we are going to embrace the new live beer definition and not worry too much about the container to an extent. So the plan is to have a bit more traditional keg, as long as they meet the live beer definition. More non-traditional real ale. Within reason of course. And the same for cider as well. We have a new cider buyer this year who really wants to start looking at more keg ciders and we want to show off that cider is not just a bag in box or a tub anymore.

And we've got access to some conference space, so we want to bring more of a trade event. We don't want CAMRA lecturing the pub and brewing industry on how they should be doing their job. We want to offer a platform to industry bodies and groups to aid their membership, so SIBA could talk to publicans about how small brewers could be good for their customers for example.

ADAM GENT, GBBF festival organiser 2025

The National Winter Ales Festival – GBBF Winter

The National Winter Ales Festival (NWAF), rebranded as the Great British Beer Festival Winter in 2018, began in 1997 with two events held in Glasgow. The next venue was the Campfield Market in Manchester, where the festival stayed for four years. From the start, the aim was to have an itinerant festival which moved around the country every few years, with CAMRA branches given the opportunity to bid to host it.

The festival came into being because CAMRA had updated its beer style categories. When the Champion Beer of Britain competition first began, there were just three styles judged – milds, bitters and strong ales. By the mid-90s, this had increased to six, with speciality, best bitters and bottle-conditioned beers added. When stouts, porters and barley wines were pulled out as new categories in their own right, it was realised that many of those beers were seasonal releases that simply would not be available to be judged in the summer at GBBF.

And so the NWAF was organised as a vehicle for judging the winter styles, although it isn't just stouts, porters, strong milds and old ales on offer for customers who attend. A full range of paler beers are also included into the beer list each year. 'Think of the Derby Roundhouse as a doughnut. Right in the centre you have all the seats and tables, then the bar goes around the outside. You've then got the external marquee with the stage in it and on to the Carriage Room where the competition beers would be, and the tail end of the brewery bars. The trick was to try and make sure that you had golden beers

Winter festival in Burton upon Trent

with names at the end of the alphabet so they could balance all the dark stuff that was in the Carriage Room.' (Gillian Hough, first female NWAF festival organiser.)

The event had settled quite comfortably in Manchester. All of the Greater Manchester branches worked together to host the event for 13 out of 15 years until 2013. The CAMRA National Executive had already informed them that the event would be passed on, with Derby selected as the next hosts. This revived the original plan and the winter festival has duly moved around the country ever since, on to

Norwich after its three years in Derby, then over to Birmingham and Burton upon Trent.

In 1996 they were trying to decide on a date for the festival to avoid clashes with other events, and I said it was easily done. Just have it for whatever week includes the 19th January. It's my birthday, and there's never a beer festival on my birthday.

I remember chatting to Graham Donning [then festival organiser] and the Manchester crew in 2011 and saying no one was sadder that NWAF was leaving Manchester than me. They asked why and I explained that it always took place around my birthday in January, however, in Derby because the venue was a college we would be tied to half term in February. They were stunned and had no idea that my birthday was why the festival was in January.

GILLIAN HOUGH, first female NWAF festival organiser

Derby Winter Ale festival 2018

At The Roundhouse in Derby, Gillian focused on adding value for guests, rather than sticking rigidly to a budget. As organiser she put on free shuttle buses from the venue to the bus station – a boon to the local pubs in the area – and upped the marketing budget to make sure the event was well publicised. She also wasn't afraid to splash out on the very best beers for the list, ensuring that by the final Derby NWAF in 2016, they reached the highest attendance figures the festival has seen, before or since, with 13,832 customers.

Gillian made up for her profligate ways by reigning in the budget in other areas. National cellar teams were sent to NWAF, for example, to support the Winter Champion Beer of Britain judging and ensure all entries were served in peak condition. Gillian issued an edict that only those signing up to work for the Friday and Saturday night sessions would have accommodation paid for – a key cost for festival organisers. This reduced the number of people claiming and also guaranteed a workforce at a time when local volunteers might be tempted to slope off and watch one of the tribute bands that were performing.

As with all festivals, sponsorship also plays an important role in providing upfront income. Learning lessons from GBBF, Gillian ensured that sponsorship packages were available for all aspects of the event: local businesses were invited to support the trade session, glasses, brewery bars, membership stall, festival t-shirt – anything they could think of.

One Thousand Volunteers

As long as what we're doing is healthy, safe and legal, because we're volunteers we're not constrained by a lot of corporate rules and targets. There is that little bit of freedom and forgiveness. It's like the only time as an adult you get to play the way you played as a child.

LAURA EMSON, serial Festival Cellar and Bar Manager

Each year at GBBF, hundreds of volunteers are thrown together to work at close quarters for extended periods. Time and time again, the

Volunteers at Bridgnorth take a moment to pose for the camera

volunteers I spoke to described GBBF as being a family, a home away from home. They come from all walks of life, and hold almost every day job imaginable between them.

With a thousand volunteers needed to make the huge festival a success, it is not surprising that the family shares its own traditions, celebrates good times and also comes together during darker moments.

There are things the public sees, like Thursday at GBBF being known as Hat Day since 2005, which does seem to be most enthusiastically embraced by those with no CAMRA affiliation. More interesting is what goes on behind closed doors.

What the public might not realise is that, behind the scenes, there is a bar just for the workers, known to all as The Volunteers Arms, or The Volly for short. The drinks may be free, but it gets relatively light use during the festival, even at the end of the day.

That is until the staff party on the final night. Once the doors close on the Saturday, the team begins the initial takedown until 9pm when they all head up for the staff party.

'A lot of the silliness at the festival occurs at the staff party,' former GBBF festival organiser Catherine Tonry tells me. 'I'll always remember one of the bar manager's food combinations: pork scratchings and custard, and pickled garlic with jelly.' Food seems to be a bit of a running joke at the staff party.

> One year at GBBF, the cider bar manager was retiring. At the staff party there's always speeches and presentations so we decided that we'd call him up. I said as he'd been running the cider bar for X number of years he was going to do blindfolded apple dunking.
>
> He knew nothing about this at all. We pulled out this bucket of water with all these apples bobbing about in it and we blindfolded him. As soon as he was blindfolded, we instantly switched the bucket to one completely full up with custard. It had been in the fridge all day. With only one apple. And he put his head straight into it. It was a pity really, because he'd had shoulder length hair, but he'd had it cut about a week before. It could have been even better.
>
> MICK LEWIS, prankster and cider bar manager

Volunteers at Leicester

The Mallet Dance

At the party, the bar managers come together to do a mallet dance which represents all the different stages of putting up a bar at the festival with the mallets being the key tool for tapping the casks. It was allegedly the brainchild of John Cornish, who invented it to counter the myth that bar managers don't actually do any work. The bar manager's position is a semi-sacred one in GBBF circles, with each bar being handed down from manager to manager like a hereditary peerage. The managers all know the family tree of how the bars have been passed down and who trained who, creating bar grandparents, parents, cousins and siblings.

The Mallet Dance is performed to the tune of Terry Wogan's *The Floral Dance*. Although the origins are somewhat lost in the mists of time, it was certainly already established tradition by the 1982 GBBF in Leeds. Each time it is celebrated it has a straight run and then a second 'shenanigans' showing, where an extra element is added for even more mirth.

In the year that Sir Terry died, the bar managers all wore Wogan masks in his honour. The dance has been performed at least once by a bar manager in a gorilla suit. Another year featured a mallet crocheted in suffragette colours. You can even chart the changing times with cider bag-in-boxes and empty key kegs featuring in more contemporary renditions.

The Mallet Dance (John Cameron-Cornish)

I've only ever seen the dance in poorly shot mobile phone videos, but it's fair to say it has a very folkish, Morris-like quality. The participants skip and twirl wielding mallets rather than sticks and hankies.

Enter in single file
Form a circle going anti-clockwise
Come together, then apart
Come together, then split into two lines
Stillage/racking
Meet, 3 bashes, then apart
Vent/spiling
Meet, 3 bashes, then apart
Tapping
Meet, 3 bashes, then apart
Tasting
Meet, 1 bash, go past
Serving
Turn & serving
Form a circle, go clockwise
Change hands, go anti-clockwise
Form into two lines
Dipping
Meet, 3 bashes, then apart
Taking down
Meet, 3 bashes, then apart
Bunging
Form a circle going clockwise
Meet, LAST ORDERS, then apart
Form a circle going anti-clockwise
Meet, TIME, end

Mallet Dance instructions provided by CHRIS ROUSE

The gently self-deprecating silliness of it all makes it rather charming, but since the dancers and their audience are all making a good dent in the free beer at The Volly by that point, it's fair to say it does get a bit raucous. While it often goes wrong, the managers are quick to accuse the stewards of sabotage rather than admit any fault themselves. I have been assured that 'rehearsals are always perfect'.

In 2017 an additional surprise element of shenanigans was organised, rehearsed and even risk assessed in deadly secret.

At the last GBBF festival organiser handover I commissioned two horse head masks for the "performance". We got the flag of Norfolk and wrapped Catherine [Tonry] up as Boudicca. Ian Hill and Marc Holmes, both of whom are enormously tall, came dancing in with the horse masks on and pulled her round in a trolley as her chariot.

Then we put Ian, the outgoing organiser, in a cage and wrapped him up with a sign that said "Faulty: back to St Albans for destruction." And we managed to do it with only about three of us being in on it, even though I had to write a risk assessment for the trolley/chariot. And Ian didn't know his moment in the cage was coming!

LAURA EMSON, GBBF Bar Manager and handmade utility kilt wearer

Table Dance

The Mallet Dance is not the only performance that one might have been lucky enough to glimpse at The Volunteer Arms during the dying hours of the Great British Beer Festival. The Table Dance was a participation dance where a caller shouts instructions to the groups assembled about round tables. In between each line there was a thunderous 'Ee aye, ee aye o' in retort from the dancers, and time was kept by the thumping of glasses on tables.

At intervals, each group puts their glasses down and picks the table up to head height and rotates it. Of course, full glasses of beer being raised into the air and then being pirouetted around does not work well for Health and Safety Officers, and so it would appear that the Table Dance may have gone the way of the dodo, having not been seen since 2017. 'Everyone starts sitting down, two hands on the table, then variations on standing, sitting, facing forward or backwards, one hand up and one hand down, picking the table up, spinning it around and of course taking it for a walk, all interspersed with taking a drink at regular intervals. Ee aye, ee aye o ...'

BUSTER GRANT, Head Brewer at Batemans

The Christian Muteau Memorial Staff Award

There is an absent friends toast and memorial wall put up at almost every CAMRA festival, where the volunteers who have passed away since the last event are remembered and celebrated. Sometimes, those who have passed are commemorated in a more unique fashion.

GBBF volunteers almost universally go beyond the call of duty, giving up so much of their free time to run the event. However, those who have made an especially noteworthy contribution are recognised with the annual Christian Muteau Memorial Staff Award. Christian was a dedicated volunteer at beer festivals around the

Christian Muteau (on right), *What's Brewing*, Feb 1985

country, as well as the much-loved voice of the GBBF tannoy for many years. A keen cricket fan, he would also relay the latest Test Match scores over the tannoy or radio at the festivals he was working.

The award was established after Christian passed away suddenly at the age of 62 in 2001. Christian's tankard was left to his old friend, Ted Eller, who decided to auction it for Christian's favourite charity, Get Kids Going! Kath Lilley collected donations at GBBF the same year, then she, Ted and Chris Cooper used the £250 raised to purchase the tankard and establish the award. It is presented each year at GBBF, with the winner decided by votes from their volunteer peers.

Any volunteer present at the festival can be nominated. The first recipient, Kevin Reeve, was unusual in that he was the only posthumous winner having died during the festival's set up, passing away peacefully but unexpectedly during the night after helping for three days.

A number of the recipients are nominated because of an amazing contribution to that year's festival. Fletch won his award in 2004 when lightning struck Olympia and a literal waterfall came down from the balcony. Fletch managed to keep The Volunteer Arms open. 'Anyone who wanted to go and get a drink still could. We might only have had a very small area of service, but he kept it going. It was that grit and determination that won it.' (Kath Lilley, co-founder of the Christian Muteau Award.)

Some winners have made a valuable contribution over a number of years, like Roy Jenner. His call sign is Bin Bag, because he set up a cleaning crew and went round to clean all the tables every day at the festival – something that simply wouldn't have happened without him.

Denny Cornell-Howarth was another winner who was recognised for her long service. She has worked at a total of 37 GBBFs, for many years behind the scenes in 'The Crypt', a slightly dingy area where all the beer deliveries were received during set-up and where all of the empty casks were stored ready for collection as the festival progresses.

> Christian was a larger than life chap, and I got on famously with him. He used to come up and stay with us to work at our local festival. I was Leeds CAMRA Chairman for a while and I helped start one of the Leeds CAMRA festivals. He used to come and be our finance person because we didn't have a huge branch. And our finance man was security too! I really, really was so fond of him.
>
> And I'm one of those, the elite band that actually won Christian's award. I'm very proud of that. I've been bar manager, technical manager, beer orderer, trainer and then in logistics as well. So I've done most of the jobs as long as it was to do directly with beer. That was my love.
>
> DENNY CORNELL-HOWARTH,
> Christian Muteau Award winner 2011

The Dave Hannan Travelling Memorial Blanket

When festival volunteer Dave Hannan passed away in November 2021, his daughter, Katie Sutton, came across hundreds of festival t-shirts in his belongings. Some of them were donated to CAMRA Games and Collectibles to be used as prizes, and others were bagged up and given to fellow festival volunteer and CAMRA National Director Laura Emson.

Laura already had form in making quilts from t-shirts for herself and for friends, so she sewed together well over a hundred 30-cm squares of logos, slogans and branding from the shirts to make the Dave Hannan Travelling Memorial Blanket. It is a whopping 7-ft tall and 5-ft wide. There were so many shirts to use that it is actually double sided and features a central panel with its name made by his daughter, Katie.

The Dave Hannan Travelling Memorial Blanket

Dave was always found napping behind the Volunteer Arms. The idea was the blanket would travel around festivals and be available for volunteers to have a sneaky little nap. It's done about ten festivals now, that Dave volunteered at. We use the steward's network to move it around and it's got its own Facebook group. I think it was cathartic for Katie and it was good for me to do something for a friend when they were going through a tough time.

The unveiling was at GBBF 2022. It was the first night in The Volly and obviously we'd only just come back from COVID. We had lost a lot of people. So even though it was about one specific person who was quite a legend at GBBF, it acted as a bit of a focus for everyone who'd lost somebody.

LAURA EMSON, Festival Cellar Manager
and a whizz with a sewing machine

The Importance of GBBF

The significance of CAMRA's Great British Beer Festival is not really its power to recruit new members or potential to (sometimes) generate a surplus. Rather, it is the intangible ripples that each GBBF sends out around the UK each year that makes the Campaign as a whole stronger. One thousand people come together to work at the event, not because they have to, but because they want to.

It's the volunteers that make the festival so enjoyable to run. When you work in a company with a thousand people working for you, half of them are only there because they need the money and the other half are only doing it because they can't find a job elsewhere. But for a thousand people to give up a week or two of their holidays, you know you're working with people who are enjoying themselves. They might have a bit of a grumble about the cost of the food, or that the accommodation is too far or whatever. But even those people who grumble kept coming back, because they enjoyed it.

MARC HOLMES, GBBF festival organiser 2002–2012

All of those people take away new knowledge, enthusiasm and strengthened friendships back to their own branches and their local festivals. GBBF provides a practical training ground for cellaring skills and festival organisation that tightens up all of the myriad of other events run by branches of the organisation.

'Volunteers at national beer festivals would make new networks of friends all around the country and be invited up to volunteer at their beer festivals. They feel they can visit anywhere in the country and eventually see someone they know.' (Mark Parkes, West Midlands Regional Deputy Director and Former GBBF Winter Organiser.)

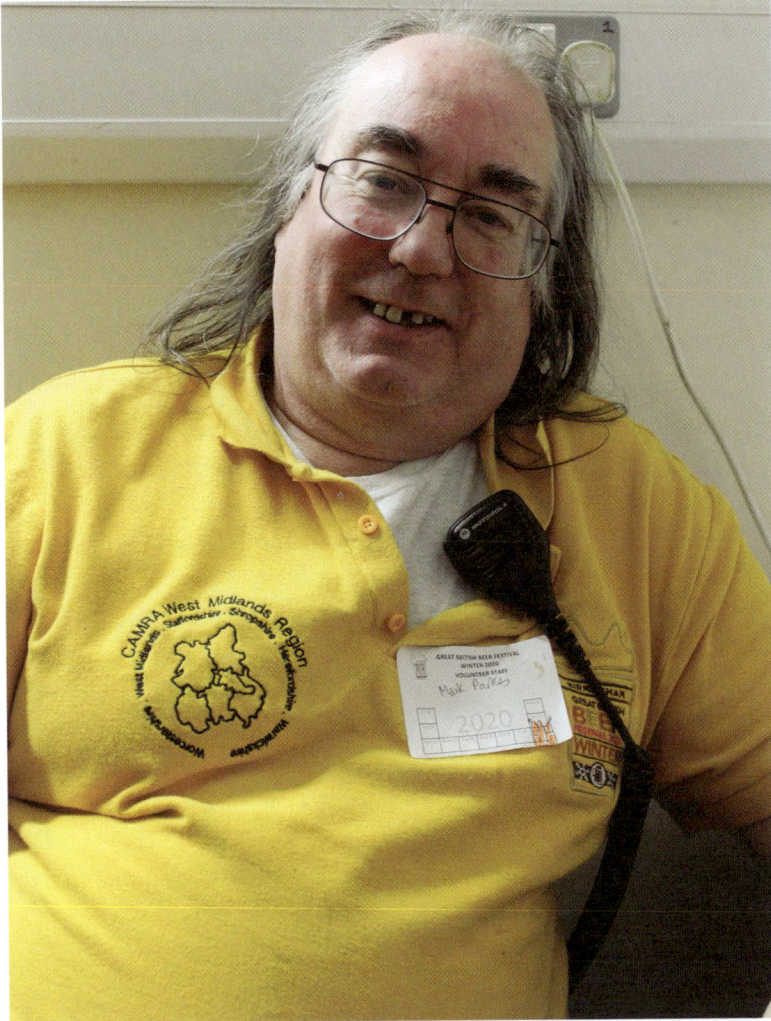

Mark Parkes

Those aren't the only relationships that are formed. Denny Cornell-Howarth's current husband went down on one knee in front of 1,000 friends and proposed at GBBF's Staff Party. What he didn't realise was that on the back of his t-shirt the motto read 'I volunteered to serve', the staff slogan that year! She doesn't let him forget that one.

Marc Holmes was festival organiser from 2002 to 2012, overseeing the move from Olympia to Earl's Court and back again. In fact, he bookended the festival's first stint at Olympia, being the first punter through the door when it opened there in 1992 and having the honour of closing the shutter on the last festival there in 2005.

> I took the job on before I had children. When I finished, I had three; an eleven-year-old, an eight-year-old and a five-year-old. It was part of the reason for giving it up really. On top of my day job it took up a lot of time.
>
> I met my wife at Lincoln beer festival in 1997. I was invited to run the cider bar and I knew her dad. He introduced us and she didn't remember me but it turned out the previous year at GBBF she had been working on a bar but wasn't feeling too well so she was told to go and steward. She was stuck on a static, basically don't let anybody in unless they've got a staff badge on. I think I was Deputy Chief Steward, just wandering around and I could see these two blokes, who were obviously a bit persistent, trying to get behind the bar. So I walked up behind the blokes, peered over their shoulder and asked if everything was alright.
>
> And then they just disappeared, because I didn't get the call sign Goliath for nothing! So that was the first time I met my wife, but I didn't know at the time. When we met properly at Lincoln Beer Festival that was when we got together.
>
> MARC HOLMES, GBBF festival organiser 2002–2012

Marc's not the only one to bring babes in arms to GBBF. There is now a third generation of children whose parents and grandparents all met through the festival.

TALES FROM THE BEER FESTIVAL

Tales from the Festival Volunteers

A collection of anecdotes, origin stories and histories from beer festivals around the UK.

Battersea and Wandle Beer Festivals

Started in 1990 in the Grand Hall of Battersea Arts Centre (formerly the Town Hall), the festival supported Battersea Dogs and Cats Home. The charity would even bring some of the dogs in to meet the punters on the quieter night at the start of the festival. They were reportedly all on their best behaviour, although the same cannot be said of all canines present. 'A blind man's dog was legless after drinking all evening, after which the taxi driver took them both home safely, I believe without asking for payment.' (Geoff Strawbridge, former CAMRA Regional Director for Greater London.)

Sadly, Battersea's ambitions were curbed by fire (the scourge of the CAMRA festival) back in 2015:

> It really was a splendid building. We had to miss a year because they were renovating the building, then half way through someone managed to set light to the roof and virtually destroyed a very lovely building. It was rumoured to be caused by someone having a quiet smoke in a corner.

It's been rebuilt, but the interior has been totally changed into an all singing, all dancing arts space, which is obviously what the arts centre wanted. But there seems to be no room for us, sadly.

TONY HEDGER, Battersea Festival Committee

In its place, a smaller festival was organised in the form of the 1st Wandle Beer Festival, held in September 2016 at Tooting & Mitcham Utd FC's KNK Community Stadium, but it only enjoyed a short run of three years.

Batersea Beer Festival

Bedford Beer Festival

'People often leave things behind at beer festivals. Usually, stuff such as glasses, company and bus passes and, of course, coats. But one year, a coat had more than just gloves in the pocket; there was £1,000 in cash (and we are talking about the 1980s). A very worried man turned up the next day to say that he had left money for a home deposit in his pocket! He was so delighted to get it all back, he joined CAMRA that day.'

CHRISTINE CRYNE, Bedford Festival Committee
founder member

Catford S.E. London Beer Festival

'Back in the 1980s, I was serving behind the bar at Catford S.E. London Beer Festival. The hall was packed with eager beer hunters and one young man was keen to catch my eye and order. This 'young guy' was perhaps 15 or 16 years old and I politely told him he was too young to be served. He went off in a huff towards the back of the beer hall. Then I noticed the atmosphere in the place hummed with excitement, and the crowd parted to allow the young man to return to the bar with his father.

'His dad was clearly a famous face, not usually seen at beer festivals. It was David Essex, pop star and actor. He asked me why I hadn't served his son? I replied that I couldn't. David Essex just shrugged his shoulders and said well just get me four pints instead. This I did, and the pair went off beers in hand.

'A little while later some other festival goers seeing Essex & Son in the hall, started an improvised song chorus of 'Hold Me Close' a big chart hit at the time. Forever the showman, David Essex joined in briefly before leaving. The Catford beer festival returned to its normal "status" afterwards.'

DAVID ROBINSON, Catford volunteer

Chelmsford Beer Festival

'It was on the Friday night of the festival. Having set up and run our brewery bar from the opening day on Wednesday, my duties were over. I carefully cashed up, recorded stock levels and left detailed instructions for the colleagues taking over the next day. With that finished, the guy who sells artisan chocolate sidled over and suggested that we do some chocolate and beer pairings. Unfortunately, easily the best pairing was the chilli-flavoured dark chocolate with Oakham Ales' Black Baron – which was 8.8% ABV.

'After fully exploring the suitability of this match, we noticed that not only were we spouting even more gibberish than usual, but that it was 3am and time to go back to the hotel. Trouble was that the site was all locked up and we could neither get out nor wake up the comatose security guy to unlock the gates. He hadn't been on the Black Baron, or so he claimed when we finally roused him. Another pint of Black Baron to celebrate our freedom and I ended up working

Chelmsford Beer Festival

on the Saturday afternoon after all – but I didn't judge myself safe and legal to drive until about 6pm!

'Incidentally, we sold 2 × 9 gallons of Black Baron (less what we drank ourselves) at that festival without ever advertising that it was on sale. This was before the days of social media but what we did was sell the first two pints of the beer to two known Essex Oakham lovers under the strict instructions that they weren't to tell anyone else that it was available. Knowing that they would immediately tell everyone that they knew.

'We had a steady stream of customers coming up to the bar and whispering conspiratorially "Any chance of a Black Baron?" To which we answered, "OK then, just this one but please don't tell anyone else".

'It sold out in a day!'

NICK JONES, Off Trade and Marketing Manager
at Oakham Ales

Horsing Around

'When I was Traffic Manager at GBBF in Olympia, I was told we needed to look after the horses. I suppose they come under traffic. There was building work round the outside at that point and these horses needed to go the wrong way round the one-way system. Myself and another steward were asked to escort – basically walk in front of them.

'The next thing I know, I'm still sort of walking quite quickly and I felt something at my heel. At the next step the horse went straight over my toe and straight over my foot. Luckily I was wearing safety shoes and I carried on, until we got round to where we were supposed to be and we got relieved.

'All of a sudden I thought, ouch, that actually hurts. I went to a colleague and said I'm gonna be a bit late taking over my team. I'm just popping to First Aid. At which point one of the customers actually came to me and asked if I'd like a hand getting over to the lift.

"Yes please!"

Well each step I took it was throbbing. I got up there and First Aid said,

"You're supposed to drop where you are if you get injured!"

"Well I couldn't do that, a horse would have gone over me," I said.

'I ended up getting taken to Charing Cross Hospital. They x-rayed it: three broken toes and one broken metatarsal. And it could have been a hell of a lot worse if I wasn't wearing safety shoes.

'Dray horses they were, Shire horses. The big ones! They'd brought them for Trade Day so the customers could see the horses at the entrance. We had Fuller's and Harvey's that year. The only reason we had to do this at all was because the first dray that turned up was at the top of the Olympia Way and the horse van caught fire. So the second lot had to come round to G Gate Yard because otherwise the smell was going to spook those horses as well!' WEDGIE, GBBF Steward

The Naughty Nook

'I've been a steward at the Great British Beer Festival for years and when we were first back here [Olympia] in 2012 the building people said you have to have an SIA [Security Industry Authority] badge steward on every external door. There's only a few of us.

'Right at the back of West Hall ground floor is a hidden fire escape that goes out to the outside and there's a big gap between the door and the fire door outside. It had to be manned, so we decided to call it the Naughty Nook. It was a nasty job. You had to be naughty to go in the naughty corner.

'We had colouring books with all different shades of orange colouring pencils because stewards wear orange. I once said to my team leader, "I'll take Naughty Nook." He said, "Not yet, I haven't finished colouring my picture!"

WEDGIE, GBBF Steward

Wedgie

Paisley Beer Festival

'I went to go up to the Glasgow branch that had a real ale festival. I thought, why can't we do that in Renfrewshire? So, in 1986, I formed the committee of the Paisley Beer Festival, which is one of the biggest festivals in the whole of Britain now. It's grown all the way from starting off not knowing what we were doing. It was really quite funny actually, because we put all the stillage up, we put the beers up, we put the handpumps on, knowing nothing about it and trying to figure it out. We'd read about it, but we'd never done it.

'The cooling was just opening windows and things like that. It was just crazy really, in those days. I remember very distinctly putting one of the casks up on the gantry and running a line from it to a handpump. And we didn't think anything of it until somebody poured a pint and then it wouldn't stop pouring. The reason it came out was gravity, but we hadn't thought of that at that time and the cask was higher than the handpump!

'That festival was a roaring success. Sold out everything by tea time on the Saturday night. We thought we had no beer left for the staff on Sunday when they were doing the breakdown. But it turned out one of my neighbours whom I'd shanghaied into helping us, who was never a member of CAMRA, told us that a beer was off, Ruddle's Bitter. He said that beer's off, I can't get anything out of it. But he hadn't turned the tap. On the Sunday when we tried to lift it off, a couple of us nearly got hernias because there was still about half the cask in it. So we all got staff beer on the Sunday.'

DEREK MOORE, Paisley Beer festival organiser

Shrewsbury Beer Festival

If the venue is of critical importance to the feel and flow of a beer festival, then the Shrewsbury CAMRA Beer and Cider Festival surely has a running start over many others. Since 2019 it has been held at the redundant Anglican church of St Mary the Virgin. It is the only complete medieval church left in Shrewsbury and is a truly breath-taking venue.

Andy Bevington is a member of the nearby Heart of Staffs CAMRA branch and was working the bar during my visit in September 2023. He agreed that the venue was something special:

'Most CAMRA branches would die for an opportunity to have a venue like this. It's very special, but it takes a lot of work to set it up. I think beer festivals like this are massively important.

ANDY BEVINGTON

Shrewsbury's festival benefits from being centrally located, with great access to public transport. There's no parking, but who wants to drive to a beer festival anyway? Transport links and central locations are one the great unsung heroes of beer festival success.

As the collected company of saints gazed down upon me from the delicately detailed windows, I was struck by a moment of revelation. Just how incredibly good the beer list was. Of course, there were the celebrated names of Shropshire brewing; Salopian, Hobsons, even the All Nations Inn – one of the last surviving brewpubs when CAMRA came into existence. But alongside them were the weird, wild and downright trendy from across the UK. This is in no small part thanks to festival sponsors, wholesalers RAD Beer, lending their expertise to the beer sourcing.

Shrewsbury Beer Festival

'Shrewsbury has always been almost an experimental beer festival, where they strive to provide beers that most people in the locality would never get the opportunity to try. It's really, really good that people get a lot of choice. There's a good balance, with local beers that you know, and the option of trying beers that you will probably never see again.' (Andy Bevington.)

Tales from the Festival Goers

Bicester Beer Festival

'When in our early twenties, myself and two other friends discovered real ale and decided to attend the Bicester beer festival. We duly set off, walking several miles to the village railway station, and caught the train to Bicester. As there was no ticket office or machine, we departed from the train not challenged for payment, which we all thought was a good omen for the day. We arrived at the beer festival in the early afternoon. It was in a field with limited cover and toilet facilities, but as it was a fine sunny day we had no concern about being rained on. We then spent the next five hours enjoying the limited but excellent range of beers. After several pints, I decided to join CAMRA. I duly signed up, bought the t-shirt and the 1974 *Good Beer Guide*.

'We had met a very friendly bunch of blokes who hired a coach from Nottingham. After socialising with them […] we told them our village had a great pub serving local Hook Norton ale. As it was only a slight diversion, would they give us a lift and they could join us for more beer in The Bell, which they agreed to.

'Our only concern was Gerry the licensee. His Hooky was not always in tip-top condition, but our fears were allayed when we had a first pint. Our new-found Nottingham friends departed and we carried on socialising with the village locals. One of my last memories of that fantastic day was drinking beer from a lady's high heel shoe which I have never repeated.'

PHIL TAYLOR, CAMRA member

A Gynaecologist Walks into a Beer Festival

'Gynaecologists are expected to enjoy gin and tonic and know about wine. Most of us manage the first without difficulty (off duty, of course) and bluff our way through the second. I have colleagues who really can tell their Pouilly Fuissé from their Pouilly Fumé, and jolly impressive they are too. It is like watching a table conjurer – entertaining but faintly irritating.

'After a few decades in the specialty the time has come for me to admit, at least to myself, that when it comes to oenophily my heart isn't in it. Wine is pleasant enough but it makes me thirsty. Real men enjoy a draught on the back of the palate. I prefer beer.

'I am the first to admit that this has its downside. Doctors do not drink at lunchtime so ale appreciation means entering public houses in the evening. In town, pubs with stripped-out interiors and names like The Old Bank or The Old Library are full of youths with their shirts hanging out. Country pubs are either twee or funereal.

'My wife and I have the perfect local. Unpretentious and English, its blackboard features Cajun chicken and Yorkshire pudding. Its amiable clientele materialises from a village that we have never actually found. I suspect that, like Brigadoon, it does not exist.

'Once a year the inn is taken over by sinister but ageing motor-cyclists. This Easter, as I edged past their leader, who was a large tattooed man with shaven head and a Genghis Khan moustache, I noticed that he was telling his leather-clad gang about his patio extension.

'Last weekend, visiting Suffolk, we happened across a regional beer festival. Among the exotically named barrels was a stall selling t-shirts: "BEER WARRIORS. RIP Oliver Reed, killed in action 1999", and "The liver is evil and must be destroyed". After years of living with health propaganda promoting the dubious attractions of longevity, I found the black humour liberating.

'Nearby, the Campaign for Real Ale (CAMRA) was staffed by bearded enthusiasts whose silhouettes hinted at their hobby. In fact, they looked rather like me, except that each wore a large cardboard hat in the shape of a beer glass.

'My wife and I scarcely hesitated. We are now life members. Not that I shall rush to tell people. I am a gynaecologist, after all.'

JAMES OWEN DRIFE, professor of obstetrics and gynaecology
(2004 extract reproduced with the kind permission of James Owen Drife and the British Medical Journal).

Pig's Ear Beer Festival

Although the East London & City branch of CAMRA was formed in 1974, they didn't hold their first beer festival until 1982, under the leadership of Christian Muteau and Ted Eller. That event took place at York Hall in Bethnal Green, which was primarily a boxing venue. The branch decided to call the festival 'Pig's Ear' – adopting the cockney rhyming slang for beer, rather than having expectations of making a disastrous mess of the whole thing.

> At that first festival in Bethnal Green, we had a proper pig! Well, we actually had two, but they didn't get on so one had to go back to the farm. But we had a proper pig for people to come and look at. Then it did what pigs do so eventually we had to take it away. That was the first time I'd seen a real live pig away from a farm. We just had it in the hall. This is the Pig's Ear so why wouldn't we have a pig? It was a good idea on paper. But we didn't repeat it.
>
> PETE LARGE, Cellar Team
> (worked the door in 1982, did not guard the pig)

By 1988, the festival had moved to Stratford Town Hall after objections were received because of the loud music. This meant that the October festival was moved to early December so as not to clash with the new venue's tea dance. After a stint at Hackney Ocean on Mare Street, the festival came to its current home in the Round Chapel, also in Hackney, in 2009. The Grade II-listed ex-Methodist Chapel makes an excellent and imposing location for a CAMRA beer festival.

'When we moved to the Round Chapel the building was used by an Ecumenical church for their Sunday services. We started setting up on the Thursday so we were advised that we would need to cover everything up in case they were offended – and to put a guard on the beer in case they helped themselves!' (Steve Hall, Pig's Ear festival organiser.)

Pig's Ear is known for its interesting beer list. It has a reputation as a 'tickers festival' – those avid beer 'collectors' who like to check off a taste of as many beers as possible. In 2022, 13 of the 175 cask ales they had were above 7% ABV – those sell quickly.

The mastermind behind this embarrassment of riches is Keen Massey, a London cabbie and festival volunteer.

I've got an extremely good beer knowledge, so I'm quite up with what's happening in the beer world. I check new breweries, see what's coming out from my favourite breweries, and find good wholesalers and distributors who can supply me with the beer. And I order all the beer for the international bar as well.

At the moment the favourites that I've tried have been the Redemption Victorian Mild at 6% and Thornbridge Kelham Island Gold Label at 9.9%, which was extremely drinkable for its ABV. But so far, I haven't drunk many – that will probably change at the end of the week.

KEEN MASSEY, Pig's Ear Beer Orderer and Bar Manager

The lure of a well-curated beer list cannot be underestimated. I met Moritz from Hamburg who had travelled to Pig's Ear with a group of friends to sample the beers. It was his 43rd such trip to a British beer festival, having fallen in love with them while studying in London more than 30 years ago. 'The range of taste is much bigger than with wine, because you've got more ingredients and you can fiddle more. The mashing, the boiling of the wort, the dry hopping; there's so much you can do with beer. It's always an experience, you've always got new beers and we love to sample them. Today there are five of us. We share all the beers and the target is to try at least 33.' (Moritz, German beer enthusiast.)

Moritz and his entourage keep a log of all the beers they try, complete with their own bespoke scoring system. Each document is carefully filed away at home in Hamburg for posterity. There are more than a hundred now, starting with Moritz's first festival, the London Drinker in Camden Town Hall in 1986.

From the description, I had expected the Log to be a new jotter with crisp blank pages waiting to be filled with notes, or perhaps a delightful artisan affair with leaves of handmade paper. Turns out it is the standard festival programme with 'LOG' written on the front in biro. But Moritz was very clear that this made it into The Official Log, which was not to be confused with any old festival programme that does not say 'LOG' on it: 'I hand it out to my friends, but never the pen. We discuss the rankings of the beers and I log them. It is very democratic, because I have the final say.' (Moritz, Holder of the Official Beer Log.)

Pig's Ear Festival 2023 with Keen Massey and Moritz from Hamburg

The Log was lost once at the Chappel Beer Festival. I asked Moritz what happened: 'My friends say they've never seen me so frantic,' he smiled. 'The Log had recorded about 100 beers and I told them if it is permanently lost then we have to try them all again.' And what was the culmination of this gripping tale? 'Well, we found it.'

Every beer festival is an adventure.

Tales from History

The Battle of Croydon

CAMRA has always kept a careful eye on the local branches who run festivals under their banner to maintain quality and to ensure that the Campaign avoids suffering financial losses. However, in 1982 a handful of renegade members went ahead with the supply of beer to a festival called 'The Battle of Croydon', organised by the local Round Table in association with The Sealed Knot reenactment society.

This event was CAMRA-sanctioned at first, being promoted in the *London Drinker,* the local branch magazine, in May and June of 1982, by July the position was muddier.

'It now seems possible that CAMRA may not, after all, be organising the beer at the Battle of Croydon.' (*London Drinker,* July 1982.)

The National Executive had become nervous about the arrangements for the event and told the group – in writing – not to proceed. But they went ahead anyway, leaving CAMRA to make up the subsequent shortfall in funds when it was a disaster. Tony Millns came into the CAMRA Chair just in time to sort out the aftermath and made reference to it in his Chairman's Report from the 1983 AGM:

'£4,429 of money paid or raised by members has had to be used to cover branch commitments. I must stress that the guidelines for beer festivals must be adhered to, and commitments should not be entered into until the national Festivals Officer, or the Executive, has given permission. There is no point in branches working hard to earn money for the Campaign, if that hard-earned cash simply has to be used to write off another branch's losses on ill-conceived ventures.' (*What's Brewing,* April 1983.)

Tony's veneer of subtle professionalism slipped somewhat when he told me about the incident, nearly 40 years later.

> To say that I was furious is an understatement. I overhauled the Articles of Association of CAMRA and introduced a new clause that anyone who brought the organisation into disrepute or did anything that was fundamentally detrimental to its interests could be thrown out from membership. And I said, "I'm going to fucking fire these guys". And I did. They appealed to the AGM and we had the most tedious meeting that I've ever had. At the end of it, some ten hours, I felt like I'd had that thing they use to kill horses put through my brain. But we won and we fired the two members who were the ringleaders.
>
> TONY MILLNS, former CAMRA Chair

This was the first time that CAMRA, a voluntary organisation, had put formal disciplinary procedures in place.

Promotion for The Battle of Croydon

Dudley Winter Ales Fayre

Beer festivals often mark an important local event, person or anniversary through their theme and logo. The 2023 Dudley Winter Ales Fayre, held at Dudley Town Hall in the West Midlands, held particular significance for locals.

The Crooked House pub in Himley, about three-and-a-half miles from Dudley, made the headlines in August 2023 after it caught fire, incinerating the roof and gutting the interior. It had been bought from Marstons by a private developer just two weeks before. Then, less than 48 hours after the inferno broke out, the remaining structure of the building was razed to the ground, allegedly unnecessarily according to the recommendations of the local planning officer.

The building, dating back to 1765, developed a characteristic lean in the 19th century, thanks to mining subsidence. It was known for producing mind-bending optical illusions thanks to its wonky angles, like marbles appearing to roll uphill. The shock demolition sparked outrage nationwide, but was felt particularly keenly by the people of the West Midlands. The Dudley Winter Ales Fayre 2023 thus took the iconic image of the Crooked House as its theme.

As someone who cares deeply about our built heritage, I felt the loss of the Crooked House keenly. Going to the festival felt like something of a pilgrimage. I'm perhaps the first to say that about Dudley.

The programme, festival glasses and volunteer t-shirts were all plastered with images of the iconic pub. The commemoration went further with a display from local model maker, Ian Young. He has started Crooked House Models since the incident and was justifiably proudly displaying his diorama models of the pub as it was, through different seasons and even during the blaze. The cotton wool smoke on the model was complemented by a makeshift smoke machine behind.

The reason I built the first one was because the Crooked House was demolished so quickly. I wanted a memento. I'd taken my wife, my parents and other visitors there over the years. But as soon as my friend saw it, he said he wanted to buy it from me – and it just snowballed from there. I've made five or six of the large models now. There's 45 hours of work in each one. This festival is the first public event that's happened to commemorate the pub and that's why it's getting so much support from the public.

IAN YOUNG, Crooked House Models

London Drinker Beer Festival

In March 1985, the first CAMRA beer festival in central London for many years was held. The London Drinker beer festival (LDBF) was at the Camden Centre just off Euston Road. It was organised by the Crynes – long-serving CAMRA power couple – with John Cryne the festival organiser (in the same year he began as GBBF festival organiser) after Christine Cryne had found the venue. They had form for initiating beer festivals, having started one in Bedford where they had lived previously and noticed that their new branch was without one when moving to London.

The LDBF was started as a quasi-regional event, nominally to provide funds to support the *London Drinker* magazine. Volunteers from across the capital got involved, but it was primarily organised by the North London branch.

They offered 15,000 pints of over 40 different beers with 'good, wholesome food', and entertainment every evening across three days. There was even a happy hour on selected beers from 5pm, something that appears relatively rare in beer festival land.

> Like a lot of beer festivals, London Drinker struggled to find logos. In 1993 Prince announced the decision to change his name to "an unpronounceable symbol whose meaning has not been identified". The Festival decided to do the same and that year's festival was known as Squiggle!
>
> When we thought the festival was going to have to stop due to the threatened hall closure we introduced De'Ath, and, in homage to Terry Pratchett, we added a cat in too. The hall didn't actually close for a few years but we continued to use the two characters for a few years, including in 2015 when Terry died. Festival visitors were delighted to commemorate Terry's life by buying a t-shirt, making it the festival's fastest seller ever.
>
> CHRISTINE CRYNE, London Drinker Beer festival organiser

By 1994 the entertainment had been dropped, it was advertised that there was 'no music at any time', but a breweriana auction was instead held every evening.

'We made it very much a showcase for London beers. Because even now it's difficult for a lot of breweries to get their beer into pubs.

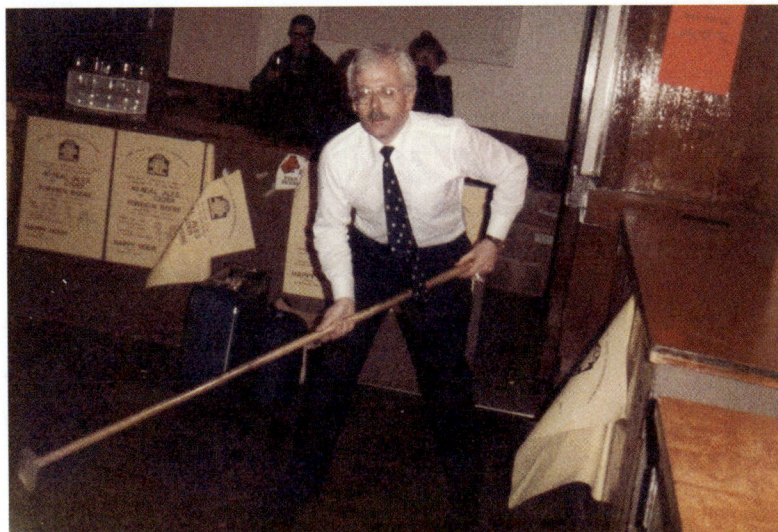

Company Secretary Iain Dobson mucking in at the London Drinker festival

It's also an income generator, of course, for CAMRA, so that's quite an important factor as well. But it mainly is about education, I think, and giving people a good time. Although there's a serious side, it's actually quite good fun.' (Christine Cryne, London Drinker Beer festival organiser.)

The Festival was eventually forced to close in 2018 after 34 years. At the time it was the longest-running London beer festival in the same venue.

Tales from the Big Guns

Stories from some of the biggest and longest-running CAMRA festivals in the country outside of GBBF. Cambridge should be in here too, but that's already been discussed in detail.

Belfast

Although by no means the biggest, the Belfast Beer Festival is the most significant CAMRA event in modern times. That is because it is one of a kind in Northern Ireland, and Ireland as a whole, in showcasing so many styles of cask beers.

The beer market in Northern Ireland is a complex issue that makes cask ale a rarity. This style of dispense is little known by the public, although the efforts of CAMRA Northern Ireland are making gradual changes.

The festival began in 1995 at the Ulster Hall and remained there until they were priced out of the venue by a massive increase in fees in 2019. The media were clearly unsure of what to expect from that first festival. Rather than bodies strewn around the Ulster Hall 'prone and prostrate' as they had anticipated, they reported on the civilised nature of the event.

'There wasn't all that much difference between an upmarket, pin-striped wine-tasting by wine buffs,' said the *Belfast News-Letter*. 'Unless it was that most of the beer addicts were dressed in a variety of cosy, comfy apparel.'

The main reason for this lack of understanding of cask ale – and the people who enjoy it – is that practically every pub is tied. Although either a pub company or the publican themselves may own the business, the taps will most likely be owned by a brewery so venues are 'tied' to a restricted choice of big brand keg beers. As a consequence, cask ale is so limited in availability that in 1997 there were estimates that the Belfast Beer Festival would serve ten times the amount of real ale than was served in all of the pubs in Belfast combined.

It reflects the situation across the United Kingdom of Great Britain and Ireland as a whole when CAMRA was first founded in 1971. But to make the situation even more difficult for independent brewers to flourish and consumer choice to triumph, there is also the 'surrender' principle.

First implemented by the Northern Ireland Parliament by the Intoxicating Liquor (Northern Ireland) Act of 1923, the 'surrender' principle began by reducing the number of outlets selling alcohol by requiring the surrender of two existing licences to a court for each new one issued. This was amended by the Licensing (Northern Ireland) Act 1971 which reduced the requirement to one licence.

The principle initially significantly reduced the number of places that could sell alcohol and now means that there are a set number of alcohol licences available. Anyone wanting to open a new pub has to buy out an old one. As a result licences can change hands for around £100,000 – not a massive problem for a macro brewer or a large pub company, but an insurmountable barrier to a fledgling business. This helps to keep the macro breweries' stranglehold over the market intact.

A review of the legislation in the mid-90s actually recommended that the requirement be discontinued, but the licensed trade and the banks objected. Those enjoying the benefits of the monopoly didn't want their position to be threatened, while many banks were holding licences as collateral for loans. Existing licensees viewed their licence as a nest egg for retirement.

These restrictions have effectively blocked the development of the real ale scene in Northern Ireland, although the number of independent breweries is growing and there is increasing pressure for reform so that more people can enjoy locally brewed beer.

> If you look at the clientele here today, the majority of them are drinking cask because this is their one opportunity in a year where there will be a wide selection of different styles to try. We hold ourselves up as the beer lovers' beer festival.
>
> The majority of the beers that are from Northern Ireland itself are keg because of the nature of the market here. We do have a couple of casks on from Boundary, which is really nice. The festival is important because it shows there's an outlet for it.
>
> RUTH SLOAN, CAMRA Northern Ireland Regional Director

Of course, the festival is also subject to licensing laws. At the Ulster Hall, the volunteers would have to obtain an occasional licence from a friendly bar and go to court to have that approved. Unfortunately, occasional licences stipulate that the sale of alcohol must be ancillary to the event, not its main focus. So the volunteers would have to convince the judge that their focus was as a charity event, not a beer festival.

Happily hosted at the Banana Block in East Belfast for its triumphant first return since the pandemic, the 2024 Belfast Beer Festival was able to use the venue's existing licence and bypass the issue. Easily one of the friendliest and most laidback CAMRA festivals I've ever been to, the organising committee were able to seamlessly integrate local culture with the selection of Northern Irish-brewed and English beers brought over for the celebration. 'On Saturday we've got a ukulele band coming. They were here at the last festival we did in 2018 and that was one of the best nights ever. They weren't amplified or anything. It was maybe twenty people with ukuleles in a corner. It just brought joy to the room. People still talk about it now. People kept coming up with the biggest smiles on their faces asking "when are you doing this again?" (Ruth Sloan, CAMRA Northern Ireland Regional Director.)

It's fair to say that Belfast is small yet mighty when it comes to the impact it is having on beer culture in Northern Ireland, although there is still a long way to go.

When I first came over here, 15 years ago, there really wasn't anywhere you could get tasty beer. The beer festival was really the only event where you could get decent beer in Northern Ireland and it was a really big thing.

The craft beer community has burgeoned since then. There are now many more brewers but they still really struggle to get their beers into pubs. And the pubs have got to the point where they're completely deskilled from cellar stuff. None of the pub owners know how to clean their own lines. It's all done for them by brewing companies, who they sign a multi-year contract with, and they can't put any other beers on.

The festival opened people's eyes to what was available and it has helped. We once had a brewer who was very new. He was brewing in his parents' farmyard at the time and on the Sunday when we were doing the takedown I had to call another volunteer over to help load the car because he'd sent his elderly mother to come and pick up the empty casks. There's no way she was lifting that! But he won Beer of the Festival that year and he's now a relatively big Northern Irish brewer.

SIMON HYDE, Belfast Beer festival organiser

Derby

Derby's festival has been running since 1978, four years after the Derby branch of CAMRA was founded.

The opportunity to run the first Derby CAMRA Beer Festival in 1978 was initiated by a phone call, answered by my wife, Les. The person on the other end said they were Secretary to the Mayor of Derby, and could they arrange a meeting with me, as branch chair, about a beer festival. I was in Nottingham and the call was so unexpected that Les assumed it was a hoax call that I had asked one of my Nottingham friends to make.

Fortunately, she did not make any inappropriate remarks. A few days later we were sitting in the Mayor's parlour being asked by the Mayor, Jeffery Tillett (who turned out to be a real ale fan) to put on a beer festival as part of the ongoing celebrations of Derby becoming a city in 1977. With his unstinting support and advice, it was a success beyond the dreams of our fledgling branch, a success that has now been repeated nearly 60 times.

TIM WILLIAMS, founder member of the Derby branch

Knowing what we know now, it was quite some leap of faith. Nothing like it had been done before, and by relatively inexperienced campaigners and event organisers. It was, however, an instant triumph.

The venue was the King's Hall, which doubled as a swimming baths. A huge, heavy floor, in panels, was laid over the pool to create an event space. Setting up a festival was a big enough task, physically, without this floor, but the job got done.

The souvenir glass from the first Derby festival is collectable, as, with demand unsure, a relatively small number were produced; subsequent festivals had many hundreds more.

I joined CAMRA at the first festival, so was involved for the second, and one thing we did to set ourselves apart was produce a daily festival newsletter, bashed out on a big, old iron typewriter in a disused office deep in the building and rushed off to the printers in the morning to be ready for punters in the evening. This was pre "desktop publishing", but we continued it for some years.

COLSTON CRAWFORD, journalist and festival committee member

Picture by RON JONES.

QUALITY CONTROL: 85-year-old Dotty Barber keeps the worried barmen waiting, before declaring that the ale was fit to drink at Derby's 11th Beer Festival.

The perfectionist pensioner is Derby's oldest regular customer, never having missed the Festival since it began in 1979. This year she was chauffeured to the opening as guest of honour.

The anxious aleman waiting for her verdict are (l-r): Reg Newcombe, Ivor Clissold, Jeff Fletcher, Mick Jones and Nick Meakin.

The festival moved to the Assembly Rooms in 1982. The venue was fairly new at the time so the council were a bit worried about beer getting on the floor. 'The solution was laborious and demanding – the bloody temporary floor, from the King's Hall, had to be fetched from storage and slotted together piece by massive piece on top of the existing floor, then sealed with tape to ensure not a drop got through. It sounds mad now, it seemed logical at the time and it fitted remarkably well in the space.' (Colston Crawford, journalist and festival committee member.)

This event proudly showcased the first bitter from the newly founded Burton Bridge Brewery. It was a successful event, despite one sour *Evening Telegraph* journalist declaring the new location to be "too posh".

The Derby festival raised the hackles of beer giant Bass in 1983 when they were criticised in the festival programme. The brewer was called out for closing down the Burton Union room which marked 'the end of an era in Burton's brewing history,' thereby forfeiting Bass's claim to be the 'Great Ale of England'. Bass's PR officer, Maurice Lovett, was reported to have exchanged some sharp words with members at the festival and later attacked the Campaign in the local evening paper and on radio, saying that any claims about the flavour of Bass changing were nonsense.

In 1989, the all-important Wednesday evening opening session of the Derby Beer Festival had to be cancelled due to industrial action. The city authorities would not allow the public into the Derby Assembly Rooms since, if the ventilation system tripped, there would be no engineers available to sort it out. We had been notified of this problem very late in the day resulting in a nightmare prospect of having to turn away hundreds of thirsty drinkers. The only things we could do were to contact our local media, and organise members to run pub crawls as a small consolation for those that turned up without being aware of the problem.

Remarkably, only a few did, illustrating the reach of local press and radio before social media. The opening session had been expected to sell 15% of the beer, but the financial disaster caused by its loss was mitigated by the introduction of the festival's first Sunday morning "drinking up" session. Even so, 400 gallons of beer had to be poured away.

TIM WILLIAMS, founder member of the Derby branch

Derby stands out for being one of the few branches that has, at times, run two annual festivals. The usual summer festival was joined by a winter event at the Darwin Suite of the Assembly Rooms in 2002. The Winter-Fest grew in popularity, but its real success was found when it moved to the Roundhouse in 2011.

> Our winter festival was a minor event to start with, but it took off as the major item. The beauty of the Roundhouse was that it was at the railway junction and it brought in people from across the UK.
>
> Well, we didn't think of that before. They were running out after the first night – calamity! But they'd got all of the lines open to local brewers for a restock. But then they ran out again and they had to repeat the thing all over again. This is the way festivals work sometimes. You just have to be reactive and face the challenge.
>
> JOHN ARGUILE, former Derby festival organiser

The winter festival was initially used as a training festival, another former festival organiser, Gillian Hough, tells me. Volunteers would have the opportunity to get trained up ready to work at the big festival in the summer. The final Winter Ale Festival took place at the Roundhouse in February 2020.

A fire in the roof put an end to the festival's time at the Assembly Rooms in 2014, more than 30 years in, and a further blow was dealt by the COVID pandemic. The Derby Winter Ale Festival finally returned in November 2024 at the city's Museum of Making.

Glasgow

Some iterations of the Scottish Traditional Beer Exhibition were held in Glasgow in the mid-80s, but it wasn't until 2014 that a serious festival was revived in the city, steered by Jonathan Kemp. The Glasgow Real Ale Festival, known as G-RAF to its friends, has a rather fetching giraffe logo, as you might expect, that has spawned a series of stuffed toy giraffe hats, which you might not.

> There were four of us from the Ayrshire branch. All four of us had done the bar managers' course and we thought we'd get a giraffe hat. This has grown over the years and every festival a new one is sewn on. So we all have a different number of giraffes on our hats

from the years we've done. We're instantly recognisable because of that. That's a good thing when you're behind the bar, because people don't always know who the bar manager is.

The giraffe hats are only seen at Glasgow Real Ale Festival, or any other festival that we work at outside of Scotland. We have visited the Bruges Beer Festival on numerous occasions. Four of us went initially to visit and then we were asked to go and work. There's some fantastic photos from Delirium Tremens, elephants and giraffes in the background. It's a bit like a zoo. At Christmas we put fairy lights around them.

We went to Morecambe Beer Festival a few years ago, which was at the Winter Garden. The four of us ended up in one of the boxes, like the royal box, and we looked like the guys off the Muppets.

I was offered €200 for my hat in Bruges. I turned it down because it's a sentimental giraffe. I could have taken the money and bought another one for 15 quid, but it wouldn't be the same. There's five of us now, we're trying to breed I think. You have to be part of the Ayrshire branch and you have to work at G-RAF. It does help to be a bar manager, but one of us is health and safety so he's honorary.

IAN MARTIN, G-RAF Bar Manager (10 Giraffes)

Ian Martin and friends with their giraffe hats

Kent Beer Festival

The Kent Beer Festival is the second oldest regularly running festival after Cambridge. From 1975 until 2014 it was organised by Gill Keay. She had visited the Cambridge event and was inspired to replicate it.

They found an appropriate site in the middle of Canterbury, Dane John Gardens. It was a very successful venue, held in a marquee and close to public transport links. The most difficult task was sourcing a stillage for the casks. In the end they made do with railway sleepers from the local station, but they were a bit low to be a permanent solution. Facilities for electricity and drains were also quite limited.

'I remember our wonderful licensee Derry Williams unblocking a drain by putting his arm deep into it and extracting the coke can that was blocking it,' Gill tells me.

There were only two breweries in Kent in 1975 when the first festival was held, Shepherd Neame and Whitbread-Fremlins, so Gill took a van around the country to pick up the best beers: up to Scotland for Belhaven, then down to Yorkshire and Manchester.

Kent Beer Festival in Dane John Gardens (courtesy of Gill Keay)

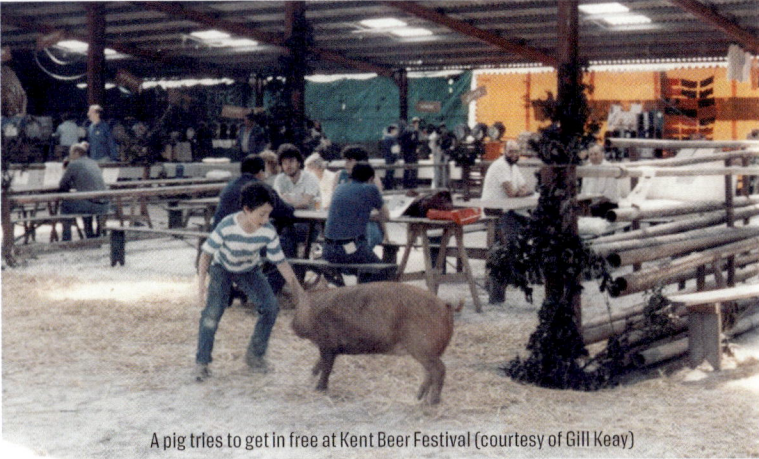

A pig tries to get in free at Kent Beer Festival (courtesy of Gill Keay)

'We get people who met at the beer festival and got married. We get people who bring their children along. Our beer festival treasurer, she once turned up with four generations. She's a great grandmother. And she brought her son and daughter along, who I remember being 18 at our second beer festival, and their children and even some little toddlers.' (Gill Keay, Kent festival organiser.)

In one notable year, the beer and stillage arrived ready for the festival to commence – but not the marquee. A mistake had arisen meaning it was ordered a day late: 'The funniest thing was the faces of people walking through the gardens and seeing a magnificent array of beers neatly stillaged in two tiers out in the open. We had to put up small tents and sleep next to the beer. The next day, the marquee staff put the old-fashioned marquee up over the beer stillage without disturbing a single cask.' (Gill Keay, Kent festival organiser.)

The festival continued happily at Dane John Gardens until 1984 when the council offices surrounding the venue were converted to residential use. For two years, there was a marquee at the Kent County Cricket Club Ground, but the cricket club got nervous about the potential for the pitch to be damaged, so the festival moved again to Woodville Halls in Gravesend. Unfortunately, this was not a success, as the Kent crowd had grown accustomed to an al fresco summer event.

Onwards and upwards, the festival spent the next 30 years at Merton Farm. Gill says it was 'notable for the smell of cow dung that permeated the whole place', but this did nothing to dampen the atmosphere.

'We started by using only half of the huge barn but the festival got bigger and bigger, and we used the whole area, which I think was 240 by 100 feet. The Friday nights were so popular, with well over 2000 customers, that we had to restrict entry to advance tickets only. We also had a couple of enormous fields for camping, which was very popular. Some staff enjoyed staying in the "Merton Hilton", a large portacabin used by occasional farm workers.' (Gill Keay, Kent festival organiser.)

Merton Farm proved popular with people from all walks of life. At the first festival there, a customer arrived in a microlight aircraft. Despite being in full morning dress ready for a wedding, the farmer insisted on being taken up for a flight. Huge parties from the local fire service and local police would attend each year. Gill discovered that one musical ensemble who performed at the festival on several occasions had actually long since disbanded, only coming back together each year because they liked playing there.

Gill retired after her 40th festival, and Andy Mitchell took over as organiser. Unfortunately, the historic Kent Beer Festival has lately struggled to find a place to call home. In 2018–19 the Canterbury Rugby Club was used as Merton Farm was no longer available. That proved expensive as they had to supply their own water, power and marquees. After a three-year break because of COVID, 2023 dabbled with a smaller festival in the King's Hall at Herne Bay. While the festival committee continued to search for a bigger venue, there was no festival in 2024.

Norwich

A stalwart of the CAMRA festival scene since 1978, the Norwich Beer Festival has an excellent reputation because of its dedication to quality. In 1991 Mitchell's brewery's Single Malt Winter Warmer Ale was voted champion in the strong ale class judged at the festival, but it was so popular with the festival's attendees that it had to be rationed to one glass per person. Conversely, in 1989, organisers decided to omit Tolly Cobbold ales from their lists after hearing complaints that their quality had declined since moving production to Hartlepool's Lion Brewery.

Undeterred by their regular venue, the St Andrew's and Blackfriars' Halls, being unavailable in 2024 during renovation works, the Norwich festival took to the streets, hosting a 'reimagined' festival with events and activities held across the city. These took the form of small beer and cider festivals in pubs, quizzes, tutored tastings, special beer launches and more besides at tens of venues across the city. This is not a huge departure for the home of Norwich City of Ale, a not-for-profit organisation that has been hosting something similar annually since 2011.

Peterborough Beer Festival

The first ever festival in August 1978 was run jointly by the local CAMRA branch and the Peterborough Rugby Club, which provided the venue. It hit the local headlines by snubbing Ruddles brewery. The CAMRA branch had decided to boycott the Langham-based brewery in protest of the sale of the Elephant and Castle pub in Peterborough, which was being taken over by Whitbread just days before the festival was due to start.

The festival has grown exponentially, which it can, within reason, as an outdoor event. In its eighth year, it moved to its current home on the Embankment. With the notable absence of GBBF in 2024, Peterborough has stepped up to become the biggest beer festival in

the country – or so the organisers claim. It depends on how you judge it really. Certainly Peterborough has the longest bar and the most visitors over its five days. Nottingham admittedly had hundreds more beers on their list.

Still, Peterborough boasts nearly 400 beers and over 100 ciders and perries. But over the 45 events they have held, the festival has grown into something more. With a lively programme of music performed on a full concert PA system and a funfair on site, it has become one of the main events in the Peterborough social calendar full stop.

The consistency and scale of the event have made it a fixture for multiple generations of local residents. Families can come along in the daytime, and the availability of a significantly sized picnic area makes it an affordable week of entertainment.

The 300 strong team of volunteers who run the festival are able to camp onsite if they wish. A staff canteen offers them hearty meals for £2, with a helping of complimentary beer. It is their selfless work that makes this massive affair viable.

'It costs an awful lot of money to put on an event like this. A commercial enterprise couldn't manage it because of the cost. But with everybody working here as volunteer staff, you haven't got a wage bill. If you had a wage bill, you'd be dead in the water. You just couldn't do it.' (Mike Lane, Peterborough festival organiser since 1985.)

Having a well-established, relatively consistent and experienced festival committee is surely one of the keys to Peterborough's success. It wasn't a conscious decision to grow into one of the biggest regional festivals, it was an organic development. The team have learned how to tame the great beast they have created and are rightly proud of it.

We stocktake very, very carefully every night. We know what we've sold. We anticipate attendance for the following day and we know if we need to reorder. I don't think we could run out of beer because we can take action to make sure there's beer left. Last year, we had 2.5% of our beer left at the end of the festival. That was probably 40 or 50 different beers. It's the only beer festival you can go to at the end and find there's more beer there than most start with!

MIKE LANE, Peterborough festival organiser since 1985

Robin Hood Beer and Cider Festival, Nottingham

Nottingham CAMRA ran several beer exhibitions in its early history. But the foundations of what is one of the most successful beer festivals in the country were well and truly laid in 1977, on the occasion of Queen Elizabeth II's Silver Jubilee. The branch, under the chairmanship of Spyke Golding, decided to hold 'The Nottingham Jubilee Beer Festival' at the Victoria Leisure Centre.

The festival took place on 13–16 October, with 29 beers and three ciders, all from Perry's of Somerset. There were three Nottinghamshire breweries represented – Hardy & Hansons, Home Brewery and Shipstones – each showcasing their bitter and their mild.

> As the 17,000 pints were drunk, the event was unanimously judged a great success. A spokesman for the organisers said, "We apologise to anyone who came late and was disappointed. The response was overwhelming and no one who saw the queues of people waiting to get in can claim there is negligible demand for real ale – traditional beer served without gas. Has anyone ever seen people do that for keg?
>
> *The Notts & Derby Drinker,* No 7 Xmas 1977

Although Nottingham is certainly one of the key regional CAMRA beer festivals, the 1986 festival was unusual in managing to secure a couple of inches of publicity in *The Daily Mirror*.

> Going back many years, our local journalists (when we used to have proper newspapers) offered to help us with publicity. One guy asked if he could write a press release for us. And he said we'd invited Samantha Fox to come and open the festival, however being a voluntary organisation we couldn't afford to pay her. But she could have as much beer as she wanted to drink. Well, this made the national newspapers. And so the guy issues a second press release saying that she'd declined to attend. But I don't think she actually got invited.
>
> STEVE WESTBY, Chair of Nottingham CAMRA

I checked in with Sam Fox, and she confirmed that while she supports all British-made products, 'it was pure speculative PR spin. As yet I have never attended any beer festivals.' An opportunity for future organisers?

Known as the Robin Hood Beer and Cider Festival since 2008, the festival has continued to grow and evolve over the years, taking in a number of unique venues. From the old Victorian swimming baths, the festival found a stately home at Nottingham Castle from 2008 until 2017. From there, it had a brief stay at the National Ice Centre. However, demand for event bookings and the scheduling of the Nottingham Panthers' Elite Ice Hockey League games meant that blocking out the venue for the necessary ten days each October became impossible post-COVID.

Luckily, a new home was found at the Trent Bridge Cricket Ground for the 2021 festival. They had been trying to lure the branch committee to move the festival there for some time. Steve Westby is the Chair of Nottingham CAMRA and has been the festival organiser for more than 30 years, overseeing all of these venue changes:

'We didn't know if it would work at Trent Bridge. One thing was clear, no way could you actually go on the cricket pitch. It's hallowed ground to them. So the festival now is held around the concourse, mostly outdoors. In the undercroft, which is a grotty piece of car park under a stand, we put up coloured lights and things in there with all the quirky, more crafty brewers and it is one of the most popular parts of the festival. Even after all these years, you always find something to develop and add to the public interest.' (Steve Westby.)

The result is perhaps the most long and winding beer festival in the whole country. In 2024 they finally got a tent out on the sacred pitch – protected by panelling of course. At most points, guests fill the corridor-like concourse, which has room for people to stand about eight deep. While open to the elements along one side, the sloping roof under the stands happily affords some protection against inclement weather. Bars are dotted along the run, with marquees and any available room housing brewery bars and more.

The serpentine nature of the layout somehow makes the festival feel more cosy and intimate than larger, single-room affairs. When I visited in 2021, the daytime session was blessed with some autumnal sunshine that made it distinctly pleasurable to enjoy a taster or two at the picnic tables which flank the concourse. The unique layout also sheltered us from the occasional blustery squall that passed by that day.

The real attraction for many is the sheer diversity of beer and cider on offer in Nottingham. The bars are managed by a cellar team of six or seven seasoned hands who have decades of experience between them. One is a retired brewer, another the award-winning landlord of the Horse & Jockey at Stapleford.

Handpumps are not used to serve the beer, because they take a lot of setting up and cleaning, not to mention slowing down service. Some of the brewery bars choose to use a mixture of gravity and hand-pump, because they staff them themselves, but all of the CAMRA bars are gravity only.

Thanks to this, the Nottingham festival has room to put on a breathtaking number of different casks. This commitment to the widest range was spearheaded by organiser Steve Westby, who thought that the Victoria Leisure Centre wasn't a particularly inspirational venue and wanted to find a way of making the festival stand out.

> I thought if people are coming for different beers, let's see how many we can get. We didn't have a lot of space in them days. It was the mid-90s when we started doing it: 200, then 300 and then 400 in 2006 as a unique selling point.
>
> When we got to Nottingham Castle, the festival expanded. It was outdoor, overlooking the entire city. We had massive marquees and we could put as many different beers on as we wanted. Very quickly we started to advertise over a thousand different real ales.
>
> STEVE WESTBY

The festival attracted the attention of the Guinness World Records in 2009, taking the record for the largest selection of real ales with 640 different beers. Numbers peaked at 1273 beers in 2016. This was much higher than even the GBBF who advertised over 900 beers in the same year. And it isn't just the ale that brings the punters in. The Robin Hood festival also has an outstanding reputation for cider and perry. They currently offer a range of more than 200 – all real ciders and perries made in the traditional way from freshly pressed fruit.

Since 2011 Nottingham has had a dedicated bar for East Midlands cider producers, giving many local makers their first opportunity to showcase their wares at a festival. Thanks to this, the festival also hosts the annual judging of the East Midlands Cider Championship, with all of the entries available on the bar for attendees to try for themselves.

With such a varied beer list, there's always something exciting to discover. Belvoir Brewery's Liquid Gold (4.1%) will be dispensed from a gold-coloured cask. It's a single-hop offering – using the Brewer's Gold variety rather than a blend.

Old Dalby brewer Colin Brown and the festival organisers are squeezing the "golden" angle for all the publicity it is worth ("the first beer in the world to be served from a golden cask – a cask that might look more at home within the walls of the Bank of England").

The hype isn't just verbal. The beer was stored last night in the vaults of a former bank, now the Beaver Tap pub in Alfreton Road; the gilt cask was due to be transferred to the Victoria Leisure Centre today by security firm Armaguard Ltd.

Nottingham Evening Post, 14 October 1998

In 2001, the newly formed Nottingham Brewery decided that they wanted to do something a little bit different to make a statement. Co-owner Phil Darby invited Steve Westby along to brew something with a distinctly Nottingham flavour. Double Jeopardy was a 4.2% golden ale brewed in the traditional manner, but with the addition of mushy peas. They added dried peas to the mash and then more in the copper along with the hops.

It did absolutely nothing to the beer, except bunged up the wort. Niven [Balfour], the other owner who did the brewing, he was up all night trying to get the beer out the pipes. It took him about five hours to transfer it to the fermentor, instead of the usual 20 minutes.

Phil then started to promote this beer as being at Nottingham Beer Festival, this mushy pea beer. And he opened a stall, before the festival, on the Market Square. He was giving out samples of this beer, inviting people to put mint sauce in it because Nottingham's thing is mushy peas with mint sauce on them [eaten traditionally at the annual Goose Fair]. This was fantastic publicity.

So when we actually had it on at the festival, he had a tub of mint sauce and told people if you have our beer, feel free to put mint sauce in it. Of course mint sauce is vinegar, and when a beer's off it stinks of vinegar. But people were still putting it in their beer!

STEVE WESTBY

The beer was allegedly named Double Jeopardy by an unnamed Notts County fan in the pub before a game and was one of a brace of questionable brewing experiments. Ty Corcoran was surprisingly enthusiastic about the legume laden offerings:

> I had a half pint of the 4.2% "Mushy Mild" in my hand. It is one of two beers brewed by the new Nottingham Brewery for the festival. A smoky dark colour, the beer gives off a pleasant "mossy" smell. It's "mild" taste was much improved by a dash of mint sauce! Not that I could taste any pea! It wasn't the best.
>
> Not so the impressive "Double Jeopardy". The peas with which it was brewed disappeared into a hoppy, crisp taste. It has a strong golden colour. Its reputation states that "if the beer doesn't get you the peas will". Not true ... yet.
>
> Both beers spoke volumes for the Nottingham Brewery and did nothing to harm their reputation as Master Brewers. It also spoke of their knowledge of how to get the best out of beer festivals.
>
> BBC Nottingham, 19 October 2001

St Albans Beer Festival

The inaugural St Albans festival was the second ever recorded CAMRA beer festival, taking place just a matter of weeks after the beer exhibition held alongside the 1974 CAMRA AGM in York. It was also the first to be open to the public, and not just paid-up CAMRA members. The Hertfordshire branch of CAMRA managed to provide 26 barrels of beer from 14 brewers – an incredible achievement when you consider the town could only boast two pubs which served real ale at that time.

> When South Herts CAMRA suggested staging a festival, people laughed and said why do you need a festival in a city with 50 pubs? The answer back then was that most of the pubs were owned by Whitbread and Ind Coope/Allied Breweries who filled them with dreadful keg beers and even worse lagers. Ind Coope did produce cask mild and bitter, but one taste of them and you moved on to Guinness.
>
> The festival was a one-day event in the Old Market Hall. Brewers were keen to cooperate and a director of Charrington's in East London took an 18-gallon cask of IPA in the back of his sports car.

Fuller's ESB and Greene King Abbot proved especially popular and the beers were sold 2p per half pint. All the beer sold out.

ROGER PROTZ, St Albans resident and beer writer

Much of the beer was collected by Neil Campbell, who spent about a week before the festival picking up the casks. All but two had been donated by the breweries, along with mats, towels and posters that were used to decorate the hall. The festival gave local landlords the necessary boost to start stocking cask ale behind their own bars again.

When the Market Hall was demolished to make way for a multi-storey car park, the festival moved around the county and between 1977 and 1980 it was held within the students union at Hatfield Poly (now the University of Hertfordshire!).

Then, in 1996 the local branch of the Lions Club charity got the Alban Arena to stage the festival there and it's been there ever since. That was a great coup as the arena is in the centre of the city and is a major entertainment venue in the region.

ROGER PROTZ

The St Albans Beer and Cider Festival is one of the biggest festivals in the country, with hundreds of beers, ciders and perries available and, like Nottingham and Peterborough, included the rarity of imported US cask ales in 2024 – something usually not seen outside of the GBBF.

The festival was an unlikely location for the filming of BBC One's The Apprentice in 2013, when Lord Sugar's hopefuls were asked to produce, brand and sell their own flavoured beer.

Tales from the Press

All Publicity is Good Publicity?

The 1995 Nottingham festival hit the headlines as it was due to be opened by actor Martin Clunes, who had been stopped for drink-driving by police in London just three days before.

CAMRA traditionalists might think him an odd choice anyway. In the popular TV comedy 'Men Behaving Badly', he has a preference not for cask-conditioned ale, but for cans of lager.

"Actually, Martin is an ideal choice because of the character he plays," says Andy Ludlow of Nottingham CAMRA.

"There's always the perennial joke about lager drinkers, but CAMRA's view is that we can now tolerate them. After all they have to pay over the odds for the privilege of drinking.

"What I do find offensive is the nasty rubbish masquerading as a proper lager in this country that is given some trumped-up Germanic name with 3.2% alcohol. That is such a big con."

Nottingham Evening Post, 18 October 1995

Botched Beer Festival in Buckinghamshire

A CAMRA beer festival due to be held at the Newport Pagnell Youth Club in August 1981 was forced to be cancelled after local landlords were angered that they could not obtain the same licensing extensions.

'We could not get afternoon extensions on the Royal Wedding Day, so why should a beer festival?' one landlord told reporters. The cancellation meant the youth club lost out on £200 of funds that would have been used for sports equipment, while the CAMRA branch had £1,500 of beer they could not sell.

The occasional licence for the festival had been granted to Jack Kaye, landlord at the Wheatsheaf in Ravenstone. He rang Northampton CAMRA two days before the event to tell them that his brewery, Charles Wells, had told him not to go ahead as he was in breach of tie – he was only permitted to sell Charles Wells beer.

Apparently, this was the result of local publicans complaining to the brewery. Other licensees were drafted in to take the licence instead, but were also strong-armed by the determined group of landlords.

Scottish Traditional Beer Exhibition

The Scottish Traditional Beer Exhibition began in 1980 in the Great Hall of the Caledonian Brewery in Edinburgh, before moving to Lorimer and Clark's Barley Store in the same city, where the doors had to be shut at times because it was so popular.

By 1984, the festival boasted '40 brews, including every Scottish-brewed ale if possible'. This shows the relative scale of the real ale scene in Scotland at the time. The seventh Bath Beer Festival, a modestly sized festival held the same week, had been able to muster 50 different real ales in its line-up.

Still, the Scottish exhibition was able to make a big impression, thanks to the inclusion of some big names.

When the laird of Traquair, Mr Peter Maxwell Stuart, had his silver wedding party, he made his own beer to celebrate the occasion – 5,000 bottles of it. Alas, there are only a few left, he tells me, but he has just embarked on producing another ale from his 18th-century brewhouse in the grounds of Traquair House.

"The Traquair symbol is a bear and that's the name I've given it," said the laird, who "uncorked" a barrel for general appreciation at the three-day Scottish Traditional Beer exhibition in Edinburgh which ended at the weekend.

It's already been put on tap for visitors to Traquair, which is Scotland's oldest inhabited home, but only on weekdays. "It's far too strong for the weekend customer," he says.

Those "silver wedding" bottles, incidentally, are likely to become collectors' items.

"It's amazing how many commemorative brews there are and some eventually command big prices, like stamps."

Edinburgh Evening News, Monday, 31 May 1982

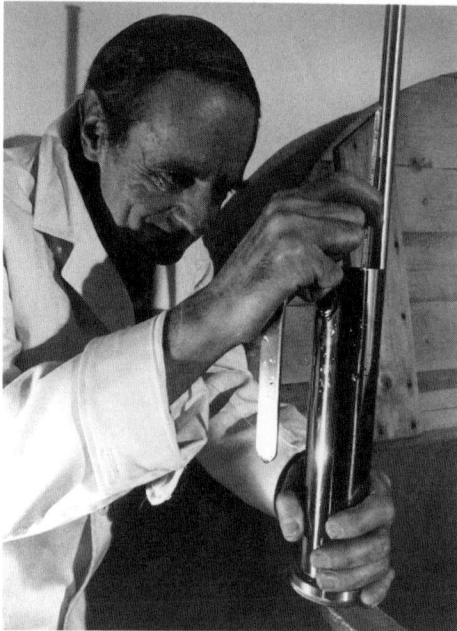

Peter Maxwell Stuart

Mr Peter Maxwell Stuart may have been a little over optimistic about the future value of his brew. A bottle of Silver Wedding Brew auctioned as part of a larger lot of five assorted bottles and six miniatures went for just £40 in 2014, and at a further in 2016 failed to meet its reserve. One reviewer on Untappd in 2017 said simply "I thought rarity was supposed to taste good."

Fordyce Maxwell offered up another lovely anecdote from another festival at the Caledonian Brewery in 1996, which the brewers revived from 1991: 'Allan Hey, now retired as the head brewer of the Yorkshire firm, Taylor's of Keighley, opened the Caledonian Brewery Beer Festival – wot? ANOTHER festival? – in Edinburgh yesterday. He did not mention that a Yorkshireman is an Aberdonian whose pockets have been sewn up, but he did mention the Yorkshire publican who hung up this sign: "Happy Hour – one for the price of two."' (*The Scotsman*, Friday, 16 August 1996.)

Wolverhampton Summer Festival of Beer & Cider

The real ale lovers of Wolverhampton used a beer festival as a way to kickstart their branch. Members of the South Staffordshire branch ran a beer tent at the West Park as part of the Wolverhampton Fiesta in 1975. It was a recruitment drive, to find the 25 people they needed to start a new branch. Sadly, while the beer was popular, they only succeeded in obtaining two sign-ups.

They tried again the next year, this time at Wulfrun Hall during the Fiesta. This was more successful, and the new branch continued to hold festivals as part of the Wolverhampton Fiesta. They were a feature of the Fiesta for more than a decade. The 1979 festival was spiced up by a visit from Italian fire-eater Alicia Maria.

But, by 1986, the branch found themselves courting controversy, as the killjoys at the Council Leisure Services Sub-Committee complained that they shouldn't be having free use of the hall for the festival. Councillor Jim Woodward incorrectly complained to the *Wolverhampton Express and Star* that CAMRA shouldn't be allowed to profit off the town.

This claim was refuted in a letter from Sue Rostance, branch treasurer, published on 21 November 1986. 'No one receives payment for their efforts, many volunteers sacrifice holiday entitlements,' wrote Sue.

Wolverhampton Low Level Festival (courtesy of Roger Harris)

'And it is the customers, most of whom are Wolverhampton ratepayers, who benefit from the free use of the Wulfrun Hall.'

This seemed to have solved the issue, at least in the medium term. The 1987 beer festival was able to go ahead as usual. After the refurbishment of the Wulfrun Hall in 2015, and when the branch were paying for the space, the venue became unaffordable and so they moved to the Newhampton Arts Centre, where the festival still takes place today. The festival has a strong following because of the local bands who perform on Friday night and throughout the Saturday session. Great music is, unsurprisingly, a strong feature of West Midlands festivals, given the region's impressive rock heritage.

CIDER FESTIVALS

The first time I remember seeing cider at a beer festival was in
Acton Park in 1975. I think it was a CAMRA festival but it was a
long time ago and I was only there as a punter. I can tell you whose
cider it was though. Horace Lancaster's [of Milton Abbot, later
Countryman Cider], which was an incredible coup at the time.
This would be the summer before Covent Garden. It opened
people's eyes to what was actually available. There was no cider
at Covent Garden, not from what I remember anyway. I suspect
it was only there because Lancaster had a connection on the
Organising Committee of the festival whose parents lived in
North Devon because you couldn't get much cider at all.

JON HALLAM, Chair of Gwent CAMRA

Cider was, theoretically at least, formally welcomed into the CAMRA
family in 1975. The Hertfordshire South branch put forward a motion,
which was duly carried, 'That real draught cider be recognised by
CAMRA as a product deserving such recognition, and that it should be
included in local good beer guides and become an area for protection.'
(1975 CAMRA AGM.)

Cider's path to recognition and campaigning support from
CAMRA was a long one, and not without opposition. In 1977 Peter
Lerner and D. Hemmings put forward a proposal that the 1975 motion

be rescinded as 'the protection of this beverage warrants no place in a campaign for real ale.' Happily for us, this was defeated and instead a follow up by Hertfordshire South supported by Reading branch was carried to include a symbol in the 1978 Good Beer Guide to highlight those rare pubs that carried draught cider.

A separate cider and perry bar first appeared at GBBF thanks to Dick Budgen. He was part of the festival working party for the 1983 festival at Bingley Hall in Birmingham. The official programme exhorts customers to 'remember that they are twice as strong as normal beers', and lists ciders available from Bulmers, Countryman, Dunkertons, Flemings, Knights, Norbury, Rich's and Westons.

Dick never relented in his quest to bring GBBF's visitors the very best UK cider. One year he decided to present ciders from as many different counties as possible as an interesting theme, just to demonstrate that it was being made in more places than was widely understood. The knock-on effect was that some of the 'beer festival pubs' – those in the immediate vicinity of GBBF – started selling a range of ciders and perries from around the country too, because they could see it was popular.

David Kitton released CAMRA's first *Good Cider Guide* in 1987, then Mick Lewis and Ed Fahey cemented cider's place in the Campaign at the 1988 AGM: 'This AGM welcomes the Campaign's increasing commitment to the cause of real cider, as evidenced by the production of the Good Cider Guide. However, if involvement is to continue, it is essential that recognition be given at a national level, and accordingly this AGM instructs the NE to set up the Apple and Pear Produce Liaison Executive (APPLE) along the lines of the Mild Marketing Board.' (1988 CAMRA AGM.)

It can be difficult to picture just how revelatory the APPLE committee's campaigning was to be. Even by 1993, after some years of campaigning for the cause, cider was still a rare beast. That year, the Darlaston Real Ale Festival committee bemoaned the fact in their programme: 'To have to travel 30 to 40 miles to drink real cider, as is the case in some parts of the country, is ludicrous.'

The APPLE committee put on three Cider & Perry Exhibitions at Stratford Town Hall, and later the Camden Exhibition Centre, beginning in 1990. Organised by Mick Lewis, rising costs in the capital made it unsustainable in the long haul, but with more than 50 ciders and perries on offer (and a couple of pins of beer too, just to keep everyone happy) it's clear that the events turned a lot of heads.

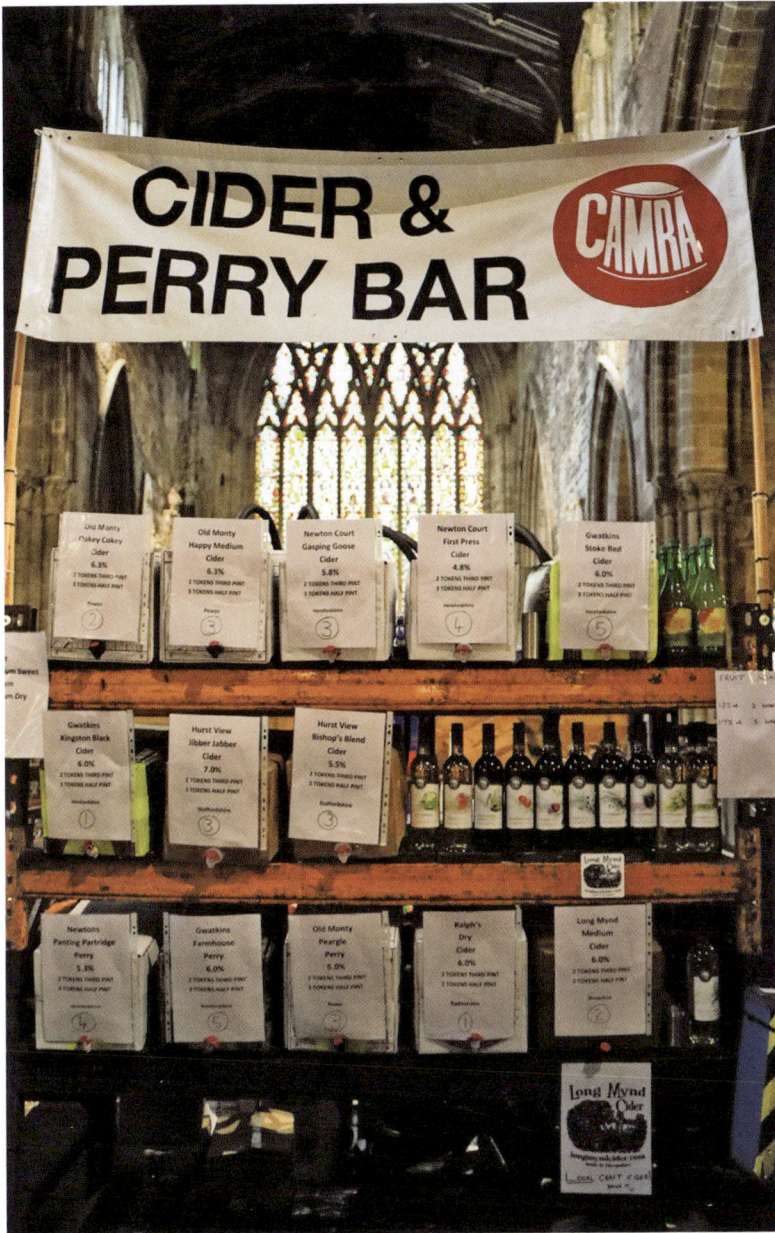

True Confessions of a Perverted Non-Cider Drinker

I joined CAMRA to support real ale. It seemed that the whole organisation would soon be swirling around in a cesspit of fermenting apple juice. In the end, there came a horrible moment when even I, myself, was seduced. What's more, it wasn't even done furtively in a dark corner of a barn. It happened in a brightly lit room, in front of vast numbers of people – an orgy, you might say.

It happened in fact at the first national Cider and Perry Exhibition. I decided finally to prove that I didn't like cider by trying a lot of them. By the end of the evening, I found I understood why some people like cider. In fact, to my horror, I even found that I quite liked it myself. If you've never done it yourself, you may not realise quite how hard it is to change an old prejudice. I mean, to have to stop being quite so rude to Mick Lewis?!? It took me a long time to come to terms with this guilty secret. But now I am happy to tell you all about it.

I still prefer beer, most of the time, but real cider is an interesting drink and I would recommend any serious real ale drinker to give this particular perverted pleasure a try. It has no lasting effects, so if you don't like it, you never need do it again.

Extract taken from Gyan Mathur's article in the *London Drinker*, May 1992

The Stockport Beer Festival became the Stockport Beer and Cider Festival in 1992, when they began presenting cider awards. It was one of the very first beer festivals to adopt this title. But they had included cider since they began in 1987.

We had a great relationship with a private cider maker, an old boy called Ted Jones from Bromyard. He was one of the last great private cider makers in the UK, strictly non-commercial. He always used to donate a tub of cider and one of perry to the festival with the proceeds to be given to charity. We raised over £1,500 over the years.

If the branch ever went to the West Country on cider trips we would stop by and see Ted on the way back. He and his friends would be making cider using an old diesel-powered mill and had wooden casks. It was a privilege to be able to glimpse into a now vanished world.

JOHN CLARKE, Chairman of Stockport
& South Manchester CAMRA

Dick Withecombe, the founder of Cider Buzz and the Manchester Cider Club, also has the benefit of the long term view about how the cider world has changed, and the role that CAMRA festivals have played.

Cider drinkers are isolated people because in the majority of pubs that we go to, there's either no cider or cider that we wouldn't wish to drink. We group together, we have networks to let each other know where you can get good cider. That network, particularly in the last five years, has grown. And that's what festivals are about. The coming together of lots of people with a common interest in pure juice, dry cider.

Cider producers used to be farm-based lonely people, with very little contact between each other. That's all changed. There's been a new generation of younger cider makers, it's a real cider revolution. They're all collaborating and helping each other.

CAMRA played an incredibly vital role in the 1980s and 1990s, particularly in helping to preserve perry as a British drink. The farm-based cider producers were in severe decline and the big producers were beginning to change. They were moving from producing genuine cider to industrial cider that was more reliant on concentrated juices.

We're probably drinking the best cider today that has ever existed, in four or five hundred years. The things I'm drinking now are way beyond anything that I would have drunk 20, 30 years ago. Cider, if nothing else, is delicious and it's joyful. It's particularly joyful because it's new and it's fresh, yet it's based on a centuries-old tradition.

DICK WITHECOMBE, Cider Buzz

The presentation of cider has evolved since that first dedicated GBBF cider bar in 1983. First producers sent along barrels, then bag-in-box became the ubiquitous dispense method. But this has a restrictive price point that isn't viable for many producers anymore. This is particularly true with perry, a drink that is rare, unique and takes time to produce.

Perry now is such a successful product again that we barely sell it to CAMRA because we don't do it in bag-in-box anymore. We put all of our perry into bottles and kegs now. Perry really succeeds in key keg with the fresh carbonation coming off the tap, it helps the drink to enrich and express itself as it's often a very floral drink with silky acidity.

But also the price point you can get when you're selling it out of a keg is so much better for the producer. That's critical because perry is facing a serious threat now because of the bacteria Fireblight. There's no economic incentive to plant new pear trees and very little imperative to maintain the existing ones if perry isn't sold for a good enough price. The hard labour of handpicking the pears, the expense of keeping the trees; all of it gets washed away.

It's fantastic that there's a few CAMRA festivals that are embracing new formats and selling keg-conditioned or bottled perry. Nottingham, Newcastle, Stockport and GBBF all do now, and it's a really good sign. There are hands reaching out from CAMRA to cider producers to find out what they should be advocating for.

ALBERT JOHNSON, Ross-on-Wye Cider & Perry

Albert's father Mike also reflects on the importance of CAMRA festivals in keeping perry alive: 'They've definitely helped with perry, because not many people bought it. CAMRA were one of the few customers of ours who bought perry in bigger quantities. Twenty years ago, we just had the farm gate sales otherwise. And now it's growing all the time.' (Mike Johnson, Ross-on-Wye Cider & Perry.)

So rare was perry at one stage, that Jon Hallam remembers people often mishearing him at festivals thinking he was recommending Perrier water. Jon took a proactive approach to spreading the good word.

At one stage we used to force it down them. Have you tried perry? No? Well here, try some. And we wouldn't let them get anything else unless they'd tried at least two mouthfuls. It's analogous to mild in an area where there was no longer any dark mild, you know. Trying to get people just to try it, at times, was quite difficult.

Perry would have died out without CAMRA because we personally stopped several people giving up making perry. Literally in some cases, having to buy it in advance.

JON HALLAM, Chairman of Gwent CAMRA

The Case of the Appearing Cat

Myself and Mick Lewis went off to collect some cider for GBBF.
We'd got this hired Luton and every now and again we'd have to
stop in the lay-by and check the load, make sure none of the poly
barrels had come loose. We're visiting six or seven cider makers.
And when we got to the last stop, which was in Gloucestershire,
we opened the roller door at the back and there's this meowing
noise. There was a cat in there. The cat stayed in Hartlands – a
chap who used to work for them part time said he'd look after it.
We phoned around everybody we'd been to and asked if they'd
lost a cat and could they ask their neighbours if they'd lost a cat –
and get back to me, because we've got this cat. But nobody knew
anything about this cat. We assumed it jumped in when we had
opened the van at one of the lay-bys, which of course could have
been anywhere. We told this chap who'd got the cat we didn't
know what we do now. "I'll keep it," he said in a thick Gloucestershire accent. And he seemed quite happy because he got a free cat.

JON HALLAM, Inadvertent Cat Whisperer

The happiness was short lived, as the mischievous feline apparently
took it upon itself to wreak havoc in its new forever home, costing the
new owner a significant amount to replace the damage within days.
So much for a free cat.

Ross-on-Wye Cider Festival

Walking down a stony dirt track to the orchards of the Ross-on-Wye
Cider & Perry Company, I knew this would be no ordinary festival.
A couple of sheep were lazily chewing on grass in a nearby field.
They eyeballed me disinterestedly as I passed. When I entered the
orchards, tents of all colours revealed themselves, peeking out cheerily
between the rows of heavily laden apple trees.

The natural fermentation cider festival has been running for 20
years now. It has grown in that time, but the temporary events licence
does not permit more than 500 guests in total, making it feel intimate
and welcoming – perhaps even a little bit exclusive, despite finding
fame on an episode of the 'Hairy Bikers' Best of British' in 2011.

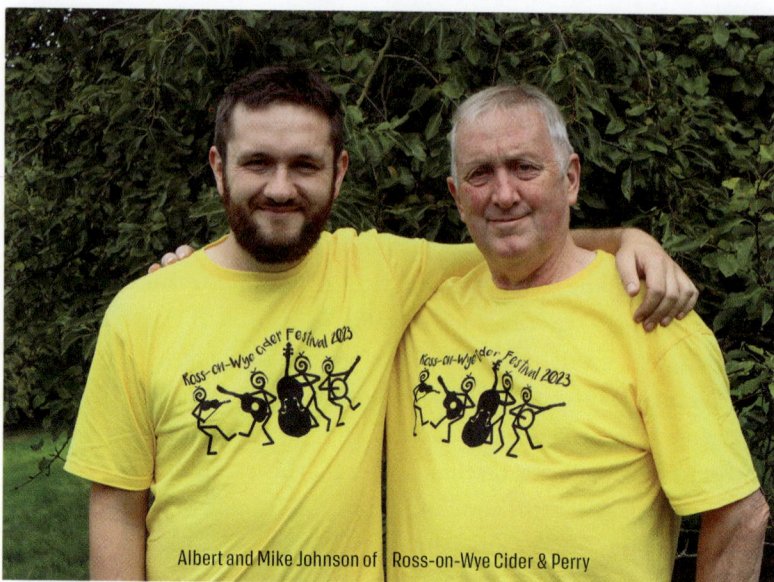

Albert and Mike Johnson of Ross-on-Wye Cider & Perry

Although it is organised by a cider producer, the Ross-on-Wye Cider & Perry Company are generous in including plenty of other cider makers in the event. Indeed, many of those producers first cut their teeth training, volunteering and learning under the shady boughs of Broome Farm.

The event has become a hub for the evolution of real cider and perry in the UK. In 2023, I was enthusiastically directed to a sunny Saturday afternoon bottle share circle amongst the pear trees. It was a veritable who's who in the cider world; from industry leading writers like Adam Wells to exciting young producers like Sam Nightingale. I felt utterly content.

I chatted to Mike Johnson of Ross Cider, the festival's founder, along with his son, Albert. We sat in some welcome shade at a table constructed from pallets. As we talked, Albert poured us a glass of Thorn, Flakey and Friends 2022 perry, one of eight new Ross-on-Wye releases launched at the inaugural night of the festival. A beautiful balance of sweetness and acidity, the rich flavour was the perfect accompaniment to our conversation about the festival and its origins.

I'd been to a couple of festivals where cider was, but the people who were serving you didn't know anything about it. I decided I'd do a festival where people could talk to the cider makers to make it more interesting. At the time, the landlord down at the Yew Tree Pub had a big marquee and said he'd put it up if I wanted to do it there. He had the concession for the food and the other drinks. About seven cider makers came with their own little tables and that's how it started.

It was a free festival in those days, and one or two of the people who came to that first one still come. It was a good way of presenting money to charity, and that got you a bit of publicity in the paper as well. We did it for two years at the Yew Tree and then for some unknown reason, he sold the marquee!

Once we started doing it at Broome Farm, we had to stop people coming in because we were going to be over our 500 limit – so we started ticketing. After that it became easier to manage because we had more money coming in. We could get more musicians and things … just make it a better festival.

MIKE JOHNSON, Ross-on-Wye Cider & Perry

One of the most attractive parts of the festival is the opportunity to camp in the orchards. The beautiful setting really makes the event feel like a fairytale escape from reality. The whole family comes along – so much so that there is now an annual dog show for four-legged attendees. When it was smaller, pressing demonstrations took place in the yard. Nowadays, one of the most popular activities is the annual Cider Club, held on the opening Thursday night. Mike's son, Albert, started to get more involved in the organising of the festival in 2018 and it was his brainchild.

It was kind of an impromptu thing. We had a monthly Cider Club at the pub that we run where we invited a guest producer to come and give a talk and a tasting. It had only been running for about five months at that point. And I begged a Canadian cider producer, Kate Garthwaite of Left Field Cider Co, to shove a few extra bottles in so we could do an international cider tasting on the opening night.

We only had 30 people come and it wasn't totally organised but I could see we had something interesting. We were adding a day to the festival where there wasn't any music. It was just about that appreciation of cider.

It's grown and this year we had 100 people there. We used it as a platform to launch our new drinks. I do a seating plan so everyone's thrown together on tables with one bottle that they all pour round and I love that. I've been to the Basque Country where that's very much the approach. If you're in a Basque cider house it's just one long bench and the food comes in the middle and gets cut up and shared between everybody, pouring the cider around.

ALBERT JOHNSON, Ross-on-Wye Cider & Perry

This spirit of community sharing runs throughout the whole festival. It is a coterie of makers and appreciaters. Many people have approached the festival from both sides of the fence, thanks to the support of the Johnsons. This includes James Finch and his wife, Cat, who started Chapel Sider in Lincolnshire in 2019. Their stall included a cider called Inspiration, dedicated to Mike and Albert in recognition of all the support they have given to the fledgling business.

A cider festival is a fantastic, atmospheric gathering of wonderful people who have a common interest in an amazing drink that's got a connection to the earth and the landscape. We started coming here to try the cider and the festival is what convinced us that it's such a lovely community to be part of.

When I was starting out my cider journey, before I'd even thought about becoming a maker, I was in the orchard here with some of the big hitters like James and Susanna from Little Pomona, Gabe Cook the Ciderologist, Mike Johnson and some people from America. We were sharing different ciders. Some of it was experimental, people had only made a couple of bottles.The opportunity to taste them, hear from the makers and be welcomed like I'd been their friend forever will always stick with me.

JAMES FINCH, Chapel Sider

Despite being one of those big hitters, Susanna Forbes told me she felt the same way, enjoying the fact that at the Ross Festival 'you get the legends conversing'. This tangible connection to the industry at all levels at the festival is now shaping the way that cider is evolving. 'This festival's changed in the last five years. It's become more of a hub. It's important that we've got the original pioneers such as James Marsden, Tom Oliver, Mike Johnson. But they are now passing on the

Ross-on-Wye cider festival, 2023 (Adam Wells on right)

baton to a whole new generation who are taking the energy of cider to a new dimension.' (Dick Withecombe, Cider Buzz.)

Albert Johnson is a warm, welcoming man who wears his expertise and his responsibilities lightly when I speak to him at the festival. But, not least in his capacity as festival organiser, he is one of the key protagonists in the great shifts we are seeing around perceptions of cider and perry.

Our festival has evolved in the same way as the rest of our business and our cider offering has evolved. From 2010 we started to bottle more cider and there was a bigger range. The festival went from being a showcase of what real cider is to being more intricate. People became more interested in discovering the individual flavours. We have a much richer landscape today than we had a few years ago. What we're selling at this festival is unrecognisable from what we sold in 2017.

It's not that we've deliberately changed anything. Cider's a seasonal thing, not a recipe driven product. It naturally evolves as you gain more information. You make minute changes to what you're producing in response to the customers. A great example is Foxwhelp. We used to be one of the only producers in the country that was making single variety Foxwhelp, but now you can buy it from a good handful of producers.This year we had a single variety Foxwhelp at GBBF.

People are learning the names of the apple varieties, which has always been our objective. There's a good consumer understanding of what Citra, Mosaic and Cascade [hops] are, and people know about their favourite grape varieties. That same base understanding of the great cider apples of Britain today doesn't exist, but it's slowly building.

ALBERT JOHNSON

But beyond all this serious business of cider education, at its heart, the Ross-on-Wye Cider and Perry Festival is just a really good party. 'They always have really great acts here. I remember a couple of years ago on the last night we were stood in the barn. Everyone was saying "one more song, one more song." They just wanted it to go on and on forever. And we were all dancing together. I can't even remember who I was with because we were just one sea of bodies in that moment. That was quite euphoric.' (James Finch.)

FESTIVAL EVOLUTION

Independent Beer Festivals

As the craft beer boom began to take hold in the UK during the early years of the 21st century, it was perhaps inevitable that a new style of festival showcasing those interesting new craft beers would evolve.

There is a tendency to call any non-CAMRA beer festival a 'craft beer festival' which maintains the false dichotomy between craft beer and cask beer. In reality, there is still really no satisfactory explanation of what 'craft beer' actually means, and the format a beer is served in does not dictate its quality. So, perhaps a non-CAMRA festival is best described simply as 'independent', a blanket term to describe a diverse spectrum of events. Some are commercial, some are more grassroots-led, raising funds for charitable causes.

Beer Exposed

The first independent event of note was Beer Exposed, organised by Des Mulcahy and Matt Roclawski of Copper Tun at Islington's Business Design Centre in late September 2008.

Des had arrived in the UK from Australia as the craft beer wave started to engulf the nation and a thirst for new and different beer styles was awakened in the population. He found himself fascinated by it, but he didn't find the way beer was presented matched the richness of what was being brewed. Observing American craft beer festivals, and having fallen in love with the wine and art fairs held at the Business Design Centre, he wanted to see if a similar concept would work for beer. 'Beer deserved better, we wanted to be the ones that did it.' (Des Mulcahy, Beer Exposed festival organiser.)

The event showcased a global range of small, independent brewers – each presenting their own stalls as part of the exhibition. Putting the brewers in front of the customer was a real point of difference from what had gone before, and offered an increasingly more beer-literate public a new kind of experience.

Beer Exposed was opened by Tony Hadley of Spandau Ballet fame, who owned shares in Suffolk's Red Rat Craft Brewery. The real star turn, however, was Garrett Oliver of Brooklyn Brewery who led a number of beer matching sessions.

Celebrated beer writer Pete Brown, who was giving tutored tastings and guided walks around the event, was excited – describing it as 'exactly what the British beer scene needs'. Others, like veteran beer blogger Jessica Boak, were a little more cynical. Although pleased to see plenty of brewers from around the world were coming along, Jessica wasn't convinced about the brave new world Beer Exposed represented, especially as there was no mention of real ale at all in the promotional material. 'The whole thing smacks a bit of "beer is the new wine" to me. There's quite a hefty entrance fee – £14 in advance, £17 on the door, which doesn't include any of the beer walks or talks.' (Jessica Boak, writing on boakandbailey.com in 2008.)

The American style admission policy, with a high entry fee in exchange for a glass and all the tasters you could sensibly manage, did seem to put off a few people. *The Londonist* reviewed the event and thought the price would put off everyone except industry folk or the 'true connoisseur'.

However, Jessica Boak went along with the open mind that she promised and found Beer Exposed to be a success, on balance, despite a rigorously enforced 9pm curfew which cut Garrett Oliver off mid-cheese and beer: 'There was definitely a different crowd to the usual beer festival bunch. A lot more women, a lot less beards, and people from a whole range of ethnic and national backgrounds. The trendy Islington location also seemed to have lured in some passing trade, including a fair few tourists and a lot of people at a loose end after work.' (Jessica Boak, writing on boakandbailey.com in 2008.)

London food blogger Cheese and Biscuits, who is not especially associated with the world of beer, wrote about the event in even more glowing terms, showing that there was real potential for this kind of event to attract a new crowd: 'It's all too easy for these festivals to turn into a corporate brewery trade fair, and the scale of the achievement of Des and Matt in resisting the pressure and money from the big boys and instead creating a gathering of unique, characterful producers is extraordinary.' (Chris Pople, writing on cheesenbiscuits.blogspot.com in 2008.)

Sadly, despite the warm reception that Beer Exposed received, circumstances conspired against it being repeated.

> There were essentially only two of us. We felt invincible, threw everything at it and lost almost everything in the process. Beer Exposed had equal measures of love and pain, enjoyment and difficulty. Most things were an educated guess. We went too big and should have curbed our enthusiasm, building from a lower base. The global financial crisis belted us, it was very real.
>
> It all ended too soon. The ambition was real, and the craft beer movement was on the cusp of exploding. We were close but I don't know that there were any lasting influences.
>
> DES MULCAHY, Beer Exposed festival organiser

London Brewers Alliance Festival

Unbeknownst to Des, at least one person took some serious inspiration from Beer Exposed and the possibilities it had raised.

The London Brewers Alliance (LBA) was formed in 2010, when 13 breweries decided to work together for the benefit of all. The key players included historic family brewers Fuller's – who had presented at Beer Exposed – and stalwarts of London's craft beer scene like Meantime and The Kernel.

Within a few months, one of the co-founders, Phil Lowry, suggested a festival at Brew Wharf, where he worked. Phil had attended and carefully studied Beer Exposed, which he describes as 'miles ahead of its time'. Like Des Mulcahy, he also drew on the American model,

London Brewers Alliance Festival

as he had seen the San Francisco Brewers Guild putting on their own events. Phil thought the key to success was having brewers to present their own beer, instead of 'bequeathing your property to someone to present your product for you'.

Like Beer Exposed, the first LBA festival, named the London Brewer's Showcase, was an all-inclusive ticket style of event.

'It's more egalitarian,' Phil explains. 'We were trying to get people to interact with the brands and try all the beer. This ticket made sure people didn't hyperfocus on one particular brewery.'

Just over 100 guests attended the first festival in 2010, and it grew much bigger in the second year. The *Londonist* reported with reservations, yet a sense of general positivity on that second festival. 'We found the space to be somewhat soulless, even by the stark no-nonsense standard of beer festivals, but this was of little consequence – this event was all about the beer, and the people who make it.' (Dave Haste, writing for *Londonist* in 2011.)

Having the brewers behind the bar, presenting their keg beers to the public, was the standout feature.

Before Beer Exposed and LBA, if you were trying to promote your brand and develop your beer it was SIBA or CAMRA [festivals] and they were all cask where you needed to rely on a good salesperson. I saw some poor cellarmanship. I judged a couple of competitions and the glass wasn't even washed properly at one of them.

Keg was on the rise and we wanted to elevate the presentation of beer. Not having all the beer coming from one packaging method allowed us to explore new niches. Brewers had flexibility in ABV, colour, flavour. Taking them away from SIBA and CAMRA allowed them to be a bit more daft, and because not all beer needs to come out of cask, we've got decent lager now.

PHIL LOWRY, London Brewery Alliance co-founder

But the road has not always been smooth for LBA and the evolution of the craft beer festival. 'We rather dropped the ball with the next festival we held,' confesses John Keeling, former Fuller's Brewing Director and the first LBA Chair. The third festival was run by Jules Whiteway-Wilkinson at his brewery tap, the now defunct London Fields Brewery.

'It was badly organised, badly run,' John says. 'Jules wanted to do everything and we were happy for him to have a go at doing it. We trusted him and we shouldn't have done. Everything was last minute and the festival was two hours late in opening.'

Beer writer and marketer Chris Hall reviewed the stricken London's Brewing on his blog:

Saturday was the first time I've seen doom-laden "Rolling News" culture collide with beer culture. Twitter on the afternoon of 4th May was a boiling tide of beer lover's anger. Increasingly frustrated reports were coming from London Fields Brewery, where London's Brewing, the new beer festival from the London Brewers Alliance (LBA), was being held.

The queues, the people cried, the queues. For a while the event didn't even open. When it did, and the queuing was over, it was reportedly even worse inside: packed bars where waiting times were said to be 30 minutes or more, and kegs hooked up to wrong taps. Above these alarming and basic errors was a weird sense of hopelessness, as though it wasn't possible for things to improve and that it was a write-off. People left in droves and demanded refunds. I've never heard of anything like this happening at a beer festival.

So imagine me, looking at Twitter on Saturday, with tickets for the session on Sunday. I was a little worried. Assurances were made that a new, extra bar would help ease queuing, and that concerns had been listened to.

I should make it clear that I had A Good Time at London's Brewing on Sunday afternoon, and that all the beer I had was well-kept and in good condition.

CHRIS HALL, writing in ChrisHallBeer.com in 2013

Once bitten, twice shy. The failures and embarrassment of the 2013 event put the LBA committee off from organising another event for a few years. But happily, they have been able to find their feet once more.

There was a gap of time where we wondered how we'd recover from that. Brew Wharf had disappeared, so we didn't have a natural venue. I suggested using Fuller's Brewery as a venue. This time we got about five or six hundred people there. We had a lot more people, but we had 50 brewers as well.

It's a great setting for a beer festival, with all the stands through the brewery yard. It's a really nice place to be, an historic brewery. A lot of the brewers who were there were based in industrial estates, but this had something to look at as well, from the building point of view.

And it just about broke even as well. But that wasn't really a problem because Fuller's, to a large extent, underwrote it. We knew even if it ran at a loss, Fuller's would support it, because it was good publicity for them to have the festival there. It's a nice part of the world to visit, so if people hadn't been to that part of Chiswick before they were pleasantly surprised.

JOHN KEELING, LBA Chair and Fuller's Global Ambassador

The festival still takes place at Fuller's Griffin Brewery. When Asahi bought the brewery in early 2019, the sale was likened to the ravens leaving the Tower of London. But, so far at least, it appears that Asahi wanted to buy Fuller's because they wanted Fuller's. Very little has changed outwardly, and Asahi underwrites the LBA festival as Fuller's had done previously. They even put their event promotions team to work helping to make the logistical arrangements and sell the tickets.

It was my first visit to the festival in mid-September 2023. We were blessed with a ferociously hot day. I think this predominantly outdoor festival would really suffer if the day were inclement. John Keeling was strolling around, chatting with people, clearly enjoying the first event in a few years where he had no organisational responsibility. 'When I was brewing, attending some events felt like an obligation. With the LBA, you want to go because you feel like you are very much a part of it.' (John Keeling, LBA Chair and Fuller's Global Ambassador.)

Fifty brewers were dotted around the brewery yard, with some food available and a relatively good selection of picnic tables for guests to sit at. The LBA boasts more than 100 brewery members these days, and given that there's no charge for them to hold a stand, I would guess that bar stands are booked quickly.

Like many festivals I have attended, the demographic lacked noticeably in ethnic diversity, but it was nice to see people of all ages and genders rubbing shoulders comfortably. I hope that as we are beginning to see more brewers of colour establishing themselves across the UK things may slowly change.

This mix of people gave the event a relaxed vibe that I really enjoyed. The daytime session was humming with life right from kick off at 12pm, and as the afternoon sauntered along, the good humour in the sunshine did not diminish. Shorts were the attire of choice, both from the brewers and the attendees. I feel like that might be a 'craft beer' thing, but the subject requires significant further research and possibly a six-figure grant from the AHRC.

Established brewers like Windsor & Eton, Anspach & Hobday and other breweries that don't have a catchy couplet in their name stood side-by-side with the newer kids on the block. I noticed a preponderance of hazy pales and variously fruited gose-style beers on offer, which may reflect the current vogue, but also suited the excellent weather. Given the fact that we were heading into autumn, those summery beers needed to go.

One of my favourite beers of the day was Toilet Block Location Shoot, one of those triple fruited gose I mentioned, which was offered by the Pretty Decent Beer Co out in Walthamstow. 'I think everyone sees a big bright red glass and wants to know what it is. We've had some really nice compliments from a lot of people.' (Alex Palfreman, Taproom Sites Manager for Pretty Decent Beer Co.)

Alex was pleased to get his beers in front of a new crowd, but it was clear the LBA festival also represents an important networking opportunity: 'It's a nice way to meet other brewers, to get to know them and set up collabs and stuff. Because everyone's so busy it's nice to have the brewers all in one place. And festivals are also good fun, it's a nice little treat for the brewery and taproom team to unwind.' (Alex Palfreman.)

The Independent Salford Beer Festival

A new template for beer festivals had been created, and across the country the opportunity to create memorable experiences was seized. One of the most well-loved is the Independent Salford Beer Festival (ISBF), first held in 2014 at St Sebastian's Community Centre. It was set up to raise money for good causes, and has been well supported by its own dedicated team of volunteers.

Organiser Jim Cullen variously describes the ISBF as a niche, DIY or grassroots festival: 'a bunch of people just doing stuff for a good local cause'. This characteristic humility downplays the great regard that the festival is held in by those that attend it – whichever side of the bar they are on.

'ISBF is one of those places where you go in as a customer and leave as a friend. Its unpretentious nature and the wonderful team of volunteers help to create a really relaxed atmosphere, and it's clear just how much everyone involved loves being a part of this event, which raises vital funds for charity. The festival encapsulates everything that I love about the craft beer community, and acts as an annual reminder that there are so many good people in the beer world.' (Daisy Turnell, Owner of Craft Beer Newcastle.)

Independent Salford Beer Festival

Brew day at ISBF

I think of all the festivals I researched for this book, none engender quite as much affection as ISBF. It is surely a contender for Britain's Best Loved Festival.

Runaway Brewery has been fortunate enough to play a small part in ISBF since its inception back in 2014. Jim and the team of volunteers have been big supporters of our brewery over the years and it always feels like a great privilege to be invited back. Like us, the festival springs from very humble beginnings and for me, it's the combination of its DIY ethos, carefully considered curation, inclusivity and strong sense of community which sets it apart. It's not that those traits are individually unique to ISBF – other festivals also hit some of those highs – but the way Jim manages to achieve *all* of those things, in one place, over one glorious weekend once a year, means it's a rare thing – a beer festival with real soul!

Year on year, Jim vows he'll never do it again – organising events like this take a very real toll – but an ISBF-shaped hole is a big hole to fill and thankfully for us, by the time spring comes around, I'm always thrilled to see *that* email land in my inbox once again.

MARK WELSBY, The Runaway Brewery

Writing in 2018, Mark Johnson beautifully summarised why being a part of the ISBF community was so special to him:

> With his gang of "merry" beer folk, Jim has created a culture untapped by too many in the industry. It sits centrally, away from the two polar extremes of beer people. It is a culture that champions good beer in many guises. It has given promotion to some of the "little" people, whether they be brewers, bar owners, bloggers or just beer people, who don't receive the same commotion or praise as others but deserve it just as much. It has discussed and highlighted some of the injustices without anger and aggression. It has created a space to make beer enjoyable.
>
> MARK JOHNSON, writing on beercompugation.co.uk in 2018

But the love that the public lavishes on some independent festivals is not always enough to have pulled them through the financial hardship of recent years. It would be remiss of me not to give the Independent Manchester Beer Conference a mention in these pages, such was the adoration it received.

The genuine wave of grief that rippled around the country at the announcement that the IndyMan Beer Con would not return in 2024 tells you everything you need to know. In 10 festivals over 12 years the organisers had, as they described it, 'brought something new and different to the craft beer market'. Set in the beautiful Victoria Baths in Manchester, the festival had an incredible reputation for presenting the boldest and most exciting side of UK beer. RIP Indyman.

Putting the Craft in CAMRA

Beyond the undeniable improvement in beer quality at CAMRA festivals, it's easy to look at photos from events in the 70s and 80s and believe that little has changed over the years; that CAMRA festivals have remained static while the new wave passes them by. But scratch the surface and you'll find that there have been some quite monumental evolutions in CAMRA-run beer festivals over the last 50 years.

When CAMRA began in 1971, a simple distinction was drawn between cask ales and keg beers. Cask was naturally conditioned, flavourful and interesting. Keg was force carbonated, fizzy and bland. It didn't take long for people to criticise this binary approach.

'It has been said that some of their members would drink castor oil if it came from a hand pump, and would reject nectar if it had no more than looked at carbon dioxide. Naturally they are at liberty to entertain whatever notions, and carry whatever motions they like, but they have often denied themselves excellent beer in the process.' (Richard Boston, *Beer and Skittles*, 1976.)

For decades now, many amazing live beers have been made purposefully for keg dispense by quality brewers. Despite this, some members of the Campaign have clung on to the outdated idea that the way a beer is dispensed dictates its worth. Keg beer was stubbornly refused a place at the CAMRA beer festival table – except on the Bière Sans Frontières bars where keg was a necessity to serve many of the international offerings, although still using air pressure rather than CO_2 for dispense.

Keg dispense had been requested for CAMRA festivals by some of the organising volunteers since at least 1996, but it wasn't formally recognised for British beer until 2012. The makers of KeyKeg – a lightweight form of keg where the gas used to pump the beer is separate from the liquid – demonstrated their product to CAMRA's Technical Advisory Group (TAG) and a blind tasting was carried out at GBBF. The Group then formally approved it as a method of dispense because it could serve real ale by the book, without the gas touching the beer.

CAMRA volunteers could now choose to include KeyKeg, and later other brands of membrane casks, on their beer lists if they wished.

> This Conference believes that Real Ale is the indigenous beer style of the UK and notes that CAMRA will continue to concentrate its beer festivals on this beer style. Conference also recognises that there are some perfectly drinkable craft beers that are not real ale, and where CAMRA is required to provide a full bar, consideration will be given to selling keg craft beers as opposed to other keg beers.
>
> CAMRA AGM 2012, motion proposed by
> Christine Cryne & Keith Spencer

A sparing number of kegs had featured on brewery-run pop-up bars at GBBF even before the TAG definition was declared. Each beer underwent a yeast viability check to ensure that it was truly a live ale. Unfortunately, not all beers met CAMRA's requirements. In 2009, the Freedom Brewery were banned from exhibiting at the Summer Beer Festival in Burton upon Trent. Since their lager needed extraneous carbon dioxide to be dispensed, there was a clear contravention of CAMRA policy.

While Freedom were diplomatic in discussing the matter with the national press, headline-hungry Scottish brewers Brewdog took a different approach. Their stall at GBBF in 2011 was cancelled at a late stage. Their keg beers met the necessary criteria but they insisted on using 30-litre kegs rather than the larger container sizes that were required. While squabbling about the rules, Brewdog decided to withhold the balance of their deposit and subsequently missed the deadline to pay for their pitch. They were characteristically vocal in their outrage at being 'unceremoniously cancelled'.

Some commentators have speculated the whole thing was orchestrated as a publicity stunt by the brewery from the start, since they wasted no time in using the incident to shout CAMRA down in the media and on their blog. They pulled a similar stunt with the Scottish Real Ale Festival organisers in Edinburgh the same year, then held their own 'alternative' Scottish Beer Festival in their bars.

But away from GBBF, quietly and without a fuss, keg beers were finding a comfortable home at smaller local CAMRA festivals.

Yvan Seth, founder of the wholesaler Jolly Good Beer, was a key player. He brought keg to the Letchworth Beer Festival 2012, where he was volunteering as the beer buyer and cellar manager.

> We got some KeyKeg from Hardknott and hooked it up to handpull with the support of Chris Overman from TAG. Chris provided the equipment. Obviously that bridged the cask/keg gap a bit – back when the weird term "KeyCask" was still doing the rounds.
>
> I built my own mobile keg dispense set-up for events in 2014 shortly after starting Jolly Good Beer [a beer wholesaler] – so when festivals started looking for ways to source and dispense keg I was pretty much ready and waiting.
>
> Going over my records it looks like the first official proper "KeyKeg Bar" I had at a CAMRA event was Stevenage Beer Festival in February 2016. Someone from Cambridge festival was at Stevenage so the bar ended up at the Cambridge fest in May 2016 too – one of the biggest fests in the country – so it got a fair bit of attention then. Then I used it at Hitchin, and word spread.
>
> As CAMRA didn't have its own keg equipment I ended up supplying the bar (and beer with it) to a handful of local regional festivals from that point. A lot of people running festivals were keen but most lacked the knowledge or equipment to dispense keg – so that's where I fit in.
>
> It was all a bit edgy in the early days. Branches like my own and Cambridge were pretty progressive but we still got negative comments, people literally coming up to the bar and dissing the "fizzy pasteurised keg beer". We tried to educate folks about it, but sometimes it was pointless. At some festivals we'd have volunteers hanging around swearing at us about it they felt so strongly.
>
> Yvan Seth, Jolly Good Beer

By 2016, the national Events Committee had also fallen into line with the TAG approval and officially approved selling keg at CAMRA festivals. This opened the floodgates for the first CAMRA-run keg bars at the festivals of the more progressive branches.

The Manchester Beer and Cider Festival was the first to have a dedicated keg bar. This was received with general delight (and relief) by the general public and beer bloggers of the time. Kaleigh Watterson, at the Ale in Kaleigh said it was 'a huge leap forward for CAMRA to welcome keg beer, albeit only certain keg beer, at one of their festivals,' although Mark Johnson writing on Beer Compurgation expressed some disappointment that the kegs were limited in number and only available on rotation.

> Our belief was that we needed to present different offerings of styles of drinks. Mainly to attract younger people and eventually get them to appreciate cask beers as well. Keg beers had changed so much over the past 10 years with many very good beers being brewed. I actually overheard some young folk saying, after having a few beers from the keg bar, "Well, OK then, let's try some of this cask beer stuff".
>
> GRAHAM DONNING, Manchester Beer and Cider
> Festival committee

This KeyKeg bar was composed of 31 × 30-litre and 6 × 20-litre KeyKegs served over 12 lines. Alongside this, Runaway Brewery – a brewery at that time dedicated to only making keg-conditioned beers – also ran the first 100% keg brewery bar. They were so popular they had to restock three times. That success proved to the organising committee that they were doing the right thing.

> Mark of Runaway became the public face of our keg experiment – partly because we positioned his bar prominently right at the front of the festival. As a result he took a fair bit of the flak from the "old school" including something like a 30-40 minute grilling from Pete Judge, one of the very long standing local members.
>
> Mark regularly recounts one tale where he spent ten minutes talking a couple of fairly anti-keg old boys through what a KeyKeg was and how keg conditioning worked. At the end of the discussion, the old boys thanked him. One set off saying he was off to get some proper beer. His mate turned round and said "I'll catch you up, I'm going to try some of this stuff."
>
> JOHN O'DONNELL, Manchester Beer and Cider
> Festival committee

Throughout early 2016, branches tinkered with the way that they presented these keg beers. By May, the 'CAMRA KeyKeg Beer Wall'

was born and launched at the Cambridge Beer Festival. In line with
the recommendations made by CAMRA HQ, this was offered as an
educational tool, with some beers available both on cask and in keg so
that drinkers could compare the two.

In August that year, veteran pub explorer Retired Martin asserted
that the highlights of the Peterborough festival all came from the
KeyKeg bar, because of the flavour but also because it 'was noticeably
less carbonated than I've had elsewhere, and frankly was a lot cooler'.

In 2018 the CAMRA Events Committee began to invest in keg
dispense systems. By 2019, they had 14 sets in total, enough to run the
first dedicated keg bar at GBBF alongside a bank of keg-led brewery
bars in the same area. It's important to note that keg was still roundly
frowned upon by some traditionalists within CAMRA, and remains
so to this day. But it was widely recognised by people who just like
nice beer as A Good Thing.

'For the whole time I was there, the KeyKeg bars were busier than
the cask bars, proving what an astute commercial decision this was ...
And guess what? The sky didn't fall in. CAMRA did not dissolve like
a vampire exposed to sunlight. The cask ales were a triumph too.'
(Pete Brown reviewing GBBF for the *Morning Advertiser*, August 2019.)

This may just be Pete's own confirmation bias – in 2019 and still in
2022, the GBBF 'live keg' bars weren't actually any busier than the other
bars. Their percentage of sales matched the regular cask bars. The keg
bar did sell out in 2023, but after a couple of cask bars already had.

I wrote up the 2019 festival on my own blog at the time. It seems
strange to think that it was only five years ago that such a momentous
change occurred. Re-reading my own words reminded me how seismic
the shift has been: 'Finally a live craft keg bar has stormed the gates
of the CAMRA stronghold. There was still a considerable amount of
heckling when mentioned at the presentation of the Champion Beer
of Britain Award. Some of it jocular, some less so. Clearly there is still
a lot of work for keg beer to do to win the hearts and minds of some
CAMRA faithful.' (Laura Hadland writing in ExtremeHousewife.com,
August 2019.)

The Campaign naysayers who argued in the early 2000s that
the introduction of KeyKeg was the thin end of the wedge were right.
And I'm really glad. These days things have mellowed considerably.

Keg walls are relatively widespread at CAMRA festivals. Some beers are occasionally dispensed with CO_2 top-pressure, and there is no longer a restriction to just membrane casks – standard steel kegs are actually more common because they are more sustainable. But as Jolly Good Beer's Yvan says, 'the reality is at any CAMRA festival I know British keg beer remains a tiny minority of the event's beer supply – cask is in no danger.'

Brewery Beer Festivals

If independent beer festivals were an evolution beyond the established CAMRA tradition, then brewery beer festivals are the next link in the chain. As taprooms became more popular and offered breweries a way to directly showcase their work to the public, brewery festivals were almost inevitable.

Not every brewery has the space to accommodate large numbers of guests on site for a day or a long weekend. As a result, brewery festivals can be said to fall very roughly into two categories – the brewery yard event and the rural escape.

The nice thing is that each festival has its own unique flavour, literally, thanks to the brewery behind it. Torrside Brewery's Smokefest, for example, has been running since 2018 and offers a range of

FyneFest

FyneFest

different styles of smoked and smoky beers, alongside a range of theme-appropriate snacks in New Mills, Derbyshire.

Equally on brand, the Little Earth Fest is steeped in the Little Earth Project's ethos. It has been running since 2022, showcasing wild and mixed fermentation beers, putting a focus on seasonality and locally sourced or foraged ingredients. All while surrounded by the glorious Suffolk countryside. There is space for guests to camp and make a little holiday out of the whole thing.

It feels like a brewery-led festival just hits differently. They tend to be more family friendly – with some notable exceptions, of course – the 5,000 capacity Dockfest run by Grimsby's Dock Beers is strictly for ages 14 and up. And I don't mean 'family friendly' in that children are merely tolerated: they are actively encouraged, with special activities laid on to keep the nippers entertained.

Like the independent festivals, one of the advantages of this breed of beer festival is that there will be brewers on hand to chat to. All these festivals bring in colleagues and friends from other breweries to showcase their beers alongside the 'house brands' and that means that these events are often some of the most hotly anticipated amongst industry folk as well as the general public.

Craft Beer Newcastle's Daisy Turnell summarised her experience at Suds with Buds, a brewery yard festival run by veterans Rooster's Brewing Co in Harrogate since 2023: '…because beer festivals aren't always about the beer ... Second year of driving to Suds with Buds, and another opportunity to see why smaller beer fests are such a great place to celebrate community, conversation, and a more relaxed, enjoyable atmosphere'. (Daisy Turnell, Owner of Craft Beer Newcastle writing on Twitter.)

One of the biggest events of the genre was Peakender, held by Thornbridge Brewery since 2014. It began as Thornbridge Outdoors near Thornbridge Hall and subsequently grew into a three-day event with full camping facilities, music, comedy and more than 200 beers on offer at the Bakewell Showground.

The downside to organising a brewery beer festival is that you're probably already pretty busy running a brewery and adding a massive event into your workflow is a hassle. Peakender 2024 fell victim to spiralling costs and a serious financial risk that could not be mitigated.

> Peakender has never been about making money for us. What started as a small event in 2014 largely for employees, friends and family at Thornbridge Hall has morphed into our largest market-ing spend each year where we accept that we are going to spend vast sums of money on promoting the brand and making sure people have fun! However, in the past two years since COVID, this cost has risen so sharply that it has led us to question if we can honestly and responsibly continue to run the event when something as simple as the weather could be financially devasta-ting in terms of recouping some of the event costs back through ticket sales and subsequent beer sales.
>
> Thornbridge Brewery statement on the Peakender website

One of the oldest brewery festivals is a rural affair much like Peakender. FyneFest began in 2010 with some 200 people heading to the Brewery Tap courtyard at Glen Fyne to celebrate the start of the summer with Fyne Ales.

> When we first started we really just wanted to celebrate what we do, the kind of place we're in. I was thinking about what I really enjoyed growing up in Argyll. Having a barbecue where the Walker's Bar is now and drinking a beer with friends. I had an uncle who was really great on the guitar and we would listen to him play.

So we wanted to see how we give that experience to a lot more people. And I wanted to try and put the festival back into beer festival. A lot of beer festivals at that time tended to be rows of cask beer under strip lights in a town hall, which are great, but we felt we could do a bit more than that. You're not just trying to entertain people for a three- or four-hour session, you're trying to entertain them for a weekend.

JAMIE DELAP, MD Fyne Ales

In 2024, 2,219 people attended the three-day event, along with 295 kids and 198 dogs. It was described on Twitter by beer writer Matthew Curtis as 'objectively the best beer event in the country'.

The guests enjoyed entertainment across a range of stages, including a delightfully busy kids tent. Even the locals, who enjoy discounted tickets, still come along to camp for the whole weekend – because realistically being local to Loch Fyne is still going to mean a half-hour drive.

Some 14,000 pints were consumed across the weekend, drawn from a choice of 72 cask ales, 144 keg beers and 39 ciders. As well as Fyne Ales, there is a carefully curated list of other brewers and cider makers to choose from. 'We're sourcing what we think are the best of UK beers and we've always got an international component. The fact that brewers come along and enjoy coming really validates what we're trying to do. For us, the beer is not on a pedestal. It's not there to be hyped and admired from below. We're trying to put beer in the middle of the table and surround it by conversation with good friends, with good food and good music.' (Jamie Delap, MD Fyne Ales.)

When I started writing this book, I thought that writing a chapter while actually at a beer festival was going to be a bit of a stretch. However, in the relaxed sunshine of the Scottish glens in the closing stages of May 2024, I couldn't resist the opportunity to jot down my thoughts at FyneFest:

I've spent a couple of hours going round the festival so far, taking in the sights and sampling a couple of beers. It is remarkable how brewery-led festivals like this really take the best of a beer festival and the best of a music festival and smash them together. Since you can camp for the whole weekend, it has a holiday feel.

There is something quite momentous about it all, you feel genuinely privileged to be here.

The location is absolutely breathtaking. The brewery, and the festival, is nestled down below the Argyll hills at the foot of the loch. It is easily the most beautiful beer festival site I have ever had the privilege to witness. It feels like you are part of something special, especially with the blessedly warm sunshine we're being treated to today. The so-chilled-its-horizontal atmosphere and the fantastic live musicians that are performing gives undeniably old school Glastonbury vibes.

The line between beer festival and music festival can certainly be very thin. But I think that something has to be said for where the organisers' focus lies. The punters here at FyneFest love the music stages, but it's the beer that has encouraged most people to choose this event over any other.

And well they might. The standout for me is the Fyne Ales offshoot, the Origins Brewing Scottish farmhouse beers, which are being showcased in their own tent for the first time. In particular I love the dark kriek, Dubh Siris, a mixed fermentation porter blended with fermented Danish Stevns juice which has matured for three months. The result is a beer laden with brooding cherry flavour, caramel and a dark kick that awakens the palate. It's interesting and complex. Certainly not something you'd expect on the bar at a music festival. What a treat.

LAURA HADLAND, somewhere in a field in Scotland, 31 May 2024

Even when the Scottish weather is less kind to FyneFest, the spirit of the festival prevails:

In 2019, there was an absolutely cataclysmic amount of rain. The pegs for the stretch tent that is the Mixtape Lounge got loose in the ground. I think I got to bed at about four in the morning of Saturday night and I was woken up by 7am – the Mixtape Lounge had just blown over and that was going to be the core of our set-up for Sunday.

It was just one really strong gust of wind and the pegs released. We thought we'd just peel back this tent which had just sort of collapsed in a pile on top of everything. By Sunday lunchtime we'd got everything cleaned up, the clouds cleared and the sun came out. Our importer in the States, Kevin, and his friend, Andy, who runs a really nice bar in Philadelphia called Teresa's, got the bar standing up and got the gas bottles out. And we're pouring Hill Farmstead and Jester King into jugs.

Sitting in the glorious sunshine in the wide open air on a comfortable sofa drinking pints of Jester King and having delicious smoked beef was just peak FyneFest. This is a festival that we really enjoy. As long as other people keep on enjoying it and keep coming to it, we're going to keep on doing it.

JAMIE DELAP, MD Fyne Ales

Pub Beer Festivals

The German Playbook

The first pub-based beer festivals were taking place while CAMRA was still in its infancy. The enterprising publicans who organised them mainly took inspiration from our friends on the Continent. Quite literally, in the case of The George in Leadenham, Lincolnshire. They were motivated to put on their own Munich-style beer festival in March 1972 thanks to the influence of the publican's new German daughter-in-law.

It took more than six months to organise that first event, because of the difficulty in sourcing a sufficient quantity of Hamburg-brewed Holsten. Their plans were clearly ambitious in scale from the outset. At first they held weekly beer festivals, but soon started plotting a three-day extravaganza just a month in. The pub team were reportedly toying with the idea of building their own Beer Keller in the pub grounds – a sawdust-floored drinking hall serving nothing but German beer and spirits.

Each of the 200 guests paid 30p for admission, which included a glass of Holsten and a nip of Schnapps. The festival was promoted to guests from age 18 to 40 and each evening some 28 gallons of the German pilsner were consumed.

While it appears that this spring of Germanic revelry in Lincoln-shire fizzled out almost immediately, the organiser, Mike Willgoose, was remarkably prescient in his observations on British drinking habits: 'Many people, especially the young, demand something different. Lager is becoming more and more popular and I think these German and Continental drinks are the coming thing.' (Mike Willgoose speaking to the *Sleaford Standard*, Friday, 17 March 1972.)

When The George held its festivals, lager accounted for less than 10% of total UK beer sales. By 1986, Holsten Pils was one of the biggest brand names around and lager was reported to have secured a 30% market share. Fast forward to 1990 and the Brewer's Society reported that lager represented more than 50% of all beer drunk in Britain, and nearly a third of all beer sold in pubs.

The first pub beer festival to gain real traction may have been the oompah Night at the Parkham Hotel in Brixham, Devon. It ran from 1981 until 1987 and was an annual sell-out. The hotel's owner, Nick Sonley, offered Munich-style food on long trestle tables, staff in Tyrolean costume and plenty of German beer. Each year there were drinking songs and dancing accompanied by an oompah band. Most fascinatingly of all, in 1983 a prize was awarded to the guest with the biggest pair of lederhosen. I don't know where one sourced oversized lederhosen in Devon in the early 80s. Ultimately though, the festivities drew to a close and the Parkham Hotel was demolished to be replaced with flats.

The CAMRA Playbook

As early as 1974, pub festivals were influenced by CAMRA. The Boughton Real Beer Festival, held at Courtenays Hotel, promised locals 'twelve hours of non-stop fun'. It had the obligatory oompah band, naturally, but the focus was British beer served straight from the cask.

It did offer some truly unique entertainments. The tug-of-war was fought in the evening with a fluorescent rope and fluorescent costumes for the competitors. The spirit of sexism was alive and well with the 'Vicars and Tarts' costume ball in the evening, where 'special prizes' were offered to the most glamorous girls, including a bottle of Champagne for the girl with the 'briefest' costume.

The longest-running pub beer festival in the country is held by The White Horse in London's Parson's Green. Their Old Ale Festival was founded in 1982 by the then-manager Mark Dorber.

Mark Dorber

The 'Sloaney Pony', as it is still affectionately known, claimed to provide an 'antidote' to early CAMRA festivals, where Mark contends the beer was not always in the best condition.

The selfish reason for the festival was that it was a good commercial opportunity to get our customers together and gather new customers into the fold. We added a category called strong ales as a general descriptor for strong bitters, porters, stouts and barley wine. It was a haven for beers that had been neglected a lot. We got people thinking about beer styles with the help of Roger Protz and Michael Jackson. After pairing some generic styles we went on to do seminars on Burton Pale Ale and India Pale Ale and brewing special beers for the festival recreating historic recipes.

We had some very cooperative wholesalers, including Martin Kemp and Rob Jones at the Pitfield Beer Shop, who went on to produce Dark Star. They were the unsung heroes behind the scenes, scouting Europe for rare bottles. Nobody else was willing to spend the time to do it. We were the only place to have all the Trappist beers in 1988 and it was a great morale boost when Michael Jackson came to the festival in 1989.

1986 was also remarkable. We had written to Peter Maxwell Stuart [The 20th Laird of Traquair] asking if we could stock his strong Scottish beer. He dropped in one Sunday lunchtime with a basket full of his beers and made a very generous offer to supply us with Tranquair House beer in cask for our festival. That was a real coup as it wasn't available on draught anywhere else in the UK. I think I drank five pints that night and I fell down the cellar stairs. I didn't feel a thing. I felt immortal that night, it was uplifting.

MARK DORBER, The White Horse until 2007

In Derby, 1988 was a pivotal year for The Brunswick Inn. They staged the first edition of their own long-running beer festival. It was held to celebrate the first anniversary of the pub's reopening after many years of closure and is still going strong.

The Brunswick was the world's first railway pub – it had been owned by Hardy & Hansons Brewery and then the Derbyshire Heritage Building Trust. They sold it on to Trevor Harris and John Evans who took possession of the place in October 1987, which dates the timing of the festival thereafter.

Of course, it was at a time when, although CAMRA were running festivals across the UK, the rest of the country was in the grip of the tied trade until the Beer Orders came along. It certainly generated a lot of other pubs wanting to copy it. Their ability to do so was restricted for a long time.

JOHN ARGUILE, pub historian and
Derby CAMRA festival committee

John makes a very good point that running a festival was a real stretch for pubs under tie. The *London Drinker* editor, Chris Cobbold, emphasised how remarkable the White Horse was in this regard: 'Last year the pub featured an "Old Ale Festival" with brews from all over the country from different breweries. All this in a Charrington tied house! How do they do it when others cannot?' (Chris Cobbold, writing in the *London Drinker*, November 1984.)

Tied pubs have never had an easy ride when it comes to putting on a beer festival that offers more than the usual, which perhaps explains why beer festivals in tied pubs are relatively scarce. An anonymous former publican explained a little about the costs involved: 'In 2010–12, I held beer festivals in Lincolnshire at a pub as a Charles Wells tenant. Although the corkage for having my beer festival was not as much as the two free-of-tie hand pulls I had, I still had to pay about £12 per cask for the 15 beers I had on in the garden. I was having to charge about £4.50 a pint. Inside the pub it was £2.50 a pint. Guinness was £2.90 at the time.'

Meanwhile, in the independent sector, running pub beer festivals was a part of the business strategy for Staffordshire's Titanic Brewery from the beginning, owing to the difficulty in getting their beer into the tied houses in the area. If you want a job doing, do it yourself.

We decided to get into pubs because we'd got nowhere to sell the beer. We bought our first pub, the Bull's Head, in Burslem in 1992 and we put guest beers on from the moment we opened the door. We thought the freehouse-style operation was the right way to go. We did that by swapping beer with our friends at other breweries so we could put a great range on.

Twice a year from when we opened, we put on a beer festival, where we put another six or eight different beers on and some live music. We would go and fetch beer from other brewers and swap beer with them. I was driving all over the country from Caledonian to Exmoor. That swapping of beer between small breweries certainly had a big effect upon how we grew.

We always considered the festivals as promotional events rather than profit making. They were a way of showing what we were doing and inviting everyone to come and join us and have a great time.

When we get into the era of pub companies [after the 1989 Beer Orders] and them trying to demonstrate that they had an open-door policy for smaller brewers, we saw the rise of lots of pub festivals and we were putting our kit up almost once a week at a different pub, cricket club or football club. We were supplying 12 beers to people who'd just never seen that sort of thing. I think that's dying off now. When there are too many pub festivals, there's not quite enough customers to go round and they start to tail off again.

KEITH BOTT, Titanic Brewery

Green Hop Festivals

The first time hops growing was recorded in Kent was at Westbere, referenced in 1523. In the mid 19th century, hundreds of thousands of east London residents would 'hop down to Kent' for a working holiday picking hops in September. George Orwell said 'no worse employment exists', but many families returned year after year for their annual outing to the country.

The Faversham Hop Festival is the longest-running contemporary celebration, enjoying a solid run, except during the pandemic, since 1990. Sponsored by Shepherd Neame, one of the key attractions is the release of their limited-edition green hop ale, Hop Pocket, at the festival. The brewers help to collect the green hops from Parsonage Farm in Boughton-under-Blean.

By the organisers' own admission, the Faversham Hop Festival has evolved and changed over the years. 'It's no longer a beer festival, Morris festival or folk festival. There are stalls but it isn't a street market or food festival. Hosts a funfair but it isn't a fairground. It's free to enter. And with all of these things, we have come to love it.' (Faversham Hop Festival.)

Green hop events have gained increasing traction. The Kent Green Hop Beer Fortnight began in 2012 and expanded into a month-long season in 2023. It includes small green hop festivals at a number of pubs and taprooms like Iron Pier and the Old Dairy Taproom which includes an independent green hop beer competition.

Steve Dunkley, Manchester Hop Project co-founder and owner of Beer Nouveau

The festival is launched each year at the Canterbury Food and Drink Festival at the Dane John Gardens. It features a tent showcasing green hops from participating Kent breweries. Unfortunately, the Food and Drink Festival decided to remove this element of the festival in 2024 with organisers reportedly having other plans for the space.

The season also encompasses the Spa Valley Railway festival, which is the largest in the county. It has been organised by the West Kent CAMRA branch in partnership with the railway trust since 2011. Each year, they select a green hop beer of the festival alongside the standard awards. They have as many as 30 green hop beers avaiable, mainly from Kent.

> Starting off as just ten casks in the engine shed, it has grown to 150 beers in three station locations across the railway site, and even beers on the trains shuttling between each station. The green-hopped beer aspect of the festival showcases Kent & Sussex grown hops picked from the bine and added to the beer within 12 hours. This true example of regional terroir is unquestionably the heart of our celebration, showcasing both local farmers, and the brewer's art.

> In recent years it has attracted the support of London breweries, and we hope to grow and raise awareness for the benefits of English hops often missed by the contemporary brewing culture looking for cost effectiveness over heart and soul.

WILL LONGMATE, Young Members Secretary, West Kent CAMRA

As Will says, Kent Green Hop Beer must meet certain criteria. It must be brewed in Kent, using only Kent-grown hops that are fresh and undried and that are used within 12 hours of picking. Hops are normally dried straight away to preserve the aroma and prevent them from breaking down. Using them fresh and green adds a different character to the finished beer.

Despite this venerable heritage in the southeast, I took myself to a surprising location to experience a green hop festival first hand – the heart of Manchester city centre. Having grown up in the region, I was fully expecting to wade through a downpour to the railway arch at 75 North Western Street. But the gods were clearly smiling on me, as it was an unseasonably warm and sunny October afternoon as I arrived at the Manchester Green Hop Festival 2023.

The festival is run by the Manchester Hop Project, a community organisation founded in 2017. Working in tandem with Beer Nouveau, then brewers and purveyors of mainly historic recipe beers, local members were encouraged to grow their own hops in the city. Many are homebrewers, excited by the idea of producing their own ingredients.

Being able to brew on a smaller scale has meant that at Green Hop Festivals since 2019, Beer Nouveau have been able to present multiple beers brewed with the amateur growers' hops on their bar. In 2023, for the first time, Track Brewery also took 25kg of the Project's hops and made an incredibly delicious golden ale – the Manchester Fresh Hop Golden Ale '23.

There are a few other hop growing collectives in the UK but I don't think they do something like this. Usually a brewery works with them and they produce one beer and put it out for general sale. We've brewed half a dozen beers or so and put them on in different formats so you can taste the difference.

It's special because amateur growers are seeing the results of their endeavours. It's anyone from people with one plant in a garden to those with an allotment and half a dozen plants. It all goes into the same collection and then we brew all these beers with it.

The collective harvesting is brilliant. The members cut down the whole bines and bring them in here. We lay them out on the tables and at one point we had about 20 people just sat down picking hops. Some of them had never met before, but Steve provides a few beers and everyone starts chatting away.

ALEX PEMBROKE, Manchester Hop Project Co-Founder

After a first, slightly chaotic year for the project's brewing endeavours, they got a bit more organised.

A few more people had heard about us who were already growing hops, so they had mature plants. Instead of getting a handful of Prima Donna here and half a kilo of Fuggles there, we started getting three kilos of Cascade, 20kg of Fuggles and 20kg of Goldings. So we made Prima Donna the main beer, but then also brewed a lot of different beers with these Manchester grown hops.

For every kilo of hops they brought in, growers got a litre of beer back with a minimum of a 330ml bottle. After a couple of years, we started doing the Hop Festival and there were six or eight different beers. Initially, we tried to keep the beers to just one or two varieties, like a West Coast with just Cascade and an Old Ale with just Goldings, so people could see how the hop itself actually worked. One year we had the same malt base for three different beers and different sorts of hops in each one.

We do have a terroir around here. There is a slight hazelnut, brazil nut flavour to every variety of hop that is grown in Manchester. So we've been able to showcase that. And now we've started blending the varieties a bit more. We're presenting the beers in different formats – wooden cask (how some of these recipes would traditionally have been served), metal cask with a handpull and sparkler, and keg. You can see how the beers differ, how the dispense affects the flavour. The wood cask works really well with the Rye PA, but with the Prima Donna it really doesn't.

A lot of the growers do it for the community aspect and for a bit of fun. Pretty much everyone loves to try a beer made with the hops that they've grown. They bring their friends in: "You've got to try this beer, it's got my hops in it!" We could run a festival where I buy some beers in from down south as well and have a big celebration, but we're keeping it local.

STEVE DUNKLEY, Manchester Hop Project Co-Founder and owner of Beer Nouveau

That community feel certainly permeates through the festival. It was a jovial atmosphere as friends met up to try the beers brewed with their hops. Throughout the afternoon, those in the know popped by before their session at Indyman, which was running the same weekend. But the fun was tinged with a light feeling of melancholy, because it was the last hoorah for Beer Nouveau and the Temperance Street Brewery in that arch. They had to vacate the premises for good at the end of October 2023, although plans were already being hatched for Track Brewery to host the event in 2024.

The members were enthusiastic about their participation in the project and keen to taste the beers:

> I like drinking beer.
> I like to pretend I know what I'm talking about.
> But to be part of it, you have to grow a bit. And the best thing is that it's all local. We're all from around here and the beer is all made from hops that we've grown.
> REBECCA, Manchester Hop Project grower

Once I'd pinpointed that hazelnut flavour Steve had told me about, I truly could discern it through all the beers – a delicate, subtle thread of character which flowed from beer to beer, and tied them all back to the hops' roots in Manchester. And growing hops there isn't as crazy as it might first sound. Hops grow best between 35 and 55 degrees latitude, because of the amount of light they need to ripen properly. The Rainy City nestles comfortably at 53.5 degrees. Prime growing territory.

The Manchester Green Hop Festival is practically indistinguishable from any other pub beer festival to the casual observer. But I found something incredibly special there. True passion for beer and the way that it is made exuded from the brewers, the homebrewers, and the growers who took part in creating the beers. There was a warm welcome from the community for outsiders like myself who were interested to have a little taste. The appetite for really tasting the difference in dispense methods was inspirational – finding the way to present each unique green hopped beer at its very best.

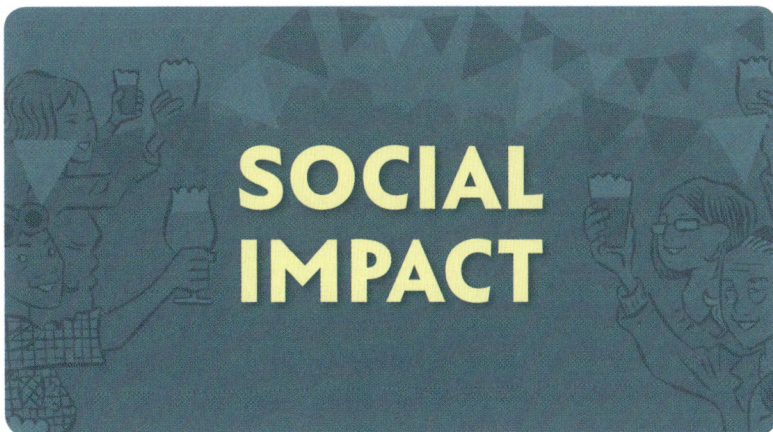

SOCIAL IMPACT

Inclusivity

Beer festivals are widely perceived as a male dominated affair, although we have happily come a long way from the overtly sexualised entertainments of 1974's Britain's Beer Festival. For CAMRA, the first national steps towards gender equality came with the appointment of the first female GBBF festival organiser, Christine Cryne, in 1992. On the local scene, women had taken leading roles from the outset, as Gill Keay's esteemed career as Kent festival organiser from 1975 until 2014 shows.

Unfortunately, women enjoying beer have often been perceived as something of a curiosity by the media.

> I stood myself a half of Hoxton Heavy and watched, with interest, as the room began to spin. A petite woman, in a pretty dress, ordered a pint of Dynamite and was still standing 10 minutes after supping it.
>
> Almost one third of CAMRA members are women. The editor of the Good Beer Guide sees nothing surprising with this. Her name is Andrea Gillies and I found her sitting in a corner, discussing the merits of her pint of porter with a male colleague.
>
> "I wouldn't say I was an authority on real ale," said Andrea, 27.

"I suppose I just know what I like. I got this job on the strength of my journalistic abilities, not my knowledge of beer."

My own journalistic abilities were becoming seriously impaired.
JULIE HEARN writing for the *Kingston Informer*, Friday, 11 March 1988

But despite women taking leading roles in the organisation of CAMRA festivals since the outset, the old stereotypes have clung on steadfastly. 'The traditional image of real ale enthusiasts as bearded, middle-aged men clad in lumberjack shirts earnestly discussing the specific gravity of Scruttock's Old Dirigible is ... well, pretty much accurate, if my perception of last week's Accrington Beer Festival is anything to go by.' (*Accrington Observer and Times*, Friday, 4 July 1997.)

Undeterred, the organisation has aimed to become more inclusive over the years. In 2014, a motion was passed at the CAMRA AGM to ensure that all branches 'take steps to ensure that all activities comply with the spirit of equality, whether this is dealing with volunteers or with others such as beer festival customers.'

A positive move, but it's hard to tell whether these fine words had any real impact. The beer blog, It Comes In Pints? reported sceptically on their visit to GBBF that year: 'The atmosphere at the festival was characteristically jolly, although the gender ratio is still way, way off (still the only place in the universe with no queue in the ladies' toilet!).' (It Comes In Pints? August 2014.)

Perhaps the watershed was GBBF 2019, when CAMRA made headlines by banning beers with discriminatory names or artwork

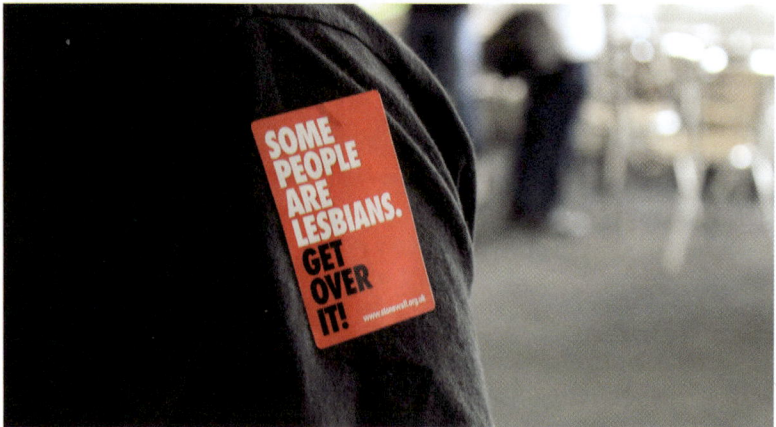

from the festival, along with choosing Diversity as its theme. In their
50th year, Stonewall, the leading LGBTQ+ support charity, was the
festival's main charity partner. It felt like a truly structural change
in festival protocol.

However, this was not the first time that sexist beer names had
been barred from a festival. Norwich Beer Festival made headlines in
1992 by doing the same thing, although perhaps not as thoroughly as
they could have.

> Willy Warmer and Brewer's Droop were omitted after protests
> from women members of the local Campaign for Real Ale branch
> – but a stout called Cockup Porter slipped through the net.
> Organiser Neil Macleod said: "It is innocently named after a fell
> in Cumbria which is called Great Cockup ... but we have to admit
> we did not realise the double meaning of the name."
>
> *Northampton Chronicle and Echo*, Saturday, 31 October 1992

Yet, for all of the talk, women are still experiencing sexist behaviour
at some festivals. Journalist Emmie Harrison-West was brave enough
to call out CAMRA festivals, and the men that attend them, publicly:

> When I was at the Great British Beer Festival in 2022, unfortu-
> nately, I was sexually harassed multiple times. For example, I was
> always served after men at the bar, even though I'd been waiting
> there longer than them. I had men move around me by touching
> my hips or by touching my breast. There was a sense of overfamil-
> iarity – that these men feel like women owe them. And unfortu-
> nately, I left feeling quite vulnerable.
>
> I shared it on Twitter and I had so many messages from
> women saying oh, wow, this has happened to me. And I had
> messages from men saying I didn't realise this behaviour was
> unacceptable – thank you for talking about it. CAMRA were
> absolutely incredible, as they always are. They've introduced
> a code of conduct for volunteers and one for festival goers, too.
>
> I think beer festivals are incredible because they unite
> everyone. They are inclusive because you're all there because you
> enjoy beer. I usually plan my year around beer festivals, so I want
> to feel like I'm included as much as the next person.
>
> EMMIE HARRISON-WEST, journalist

To address these issues, CAMRA undertook a significant Inclusion, Equality and Diversity Review over two years. Even before that was completed, the Festival Code of Conduct was drawn up and implemented in response to the feedback from GBBF 2022 and guidance for creating an inclusive festival was made available online for volunteers. Independent festivals are increasingly setting out clear expectations for behaviour on their websites too.

Having a clear policy and zero-tolerance approach is a good start in creating an inclusive event – removing the perpetrators and not the victims, which, as Emmie pointed out to me, is a serious limitation with the Ask for Angela scheme, where victims are encouraged to subtly request help, support or a safe route off the premises from the staff behind a bar.

The Coven

But one group has looked for a more positive approach to making festivals safe and inclusive – and to look to quell any trouble before it starts. Pip Young is the founder of 30SixCo, a company that provides diversity and inclusivity training. One of their best known services are Wellness Officers, run through a project called The Coven.

Inspired by the outpouring of harrowing tales from women working in the beer industry on social media in 2020, Pip wanted to play a role in addressing the iniquity that she and her female and femme peers were experiencing. The Coven was launched at the Leeds International Beer Festival in 2021.

> Leaning into the mythos of brewsters and the fairytale witch for branding, I created a space where (initially) women brewers and owners could be platformed, promoted and partnered with. Aiming to showcase their talents and help them receive a spotlight on their outstanding products.
>
> Since conception however, we've adjusted the wording surrounding our mission to reach more "otherised' folk, with an aim to serve all. I, personally, started with what I knew; women in beer, but the ideal of creating an inclusive space cannot start from one of exclusion.
>
> PIP YOUNG, 30SixCo

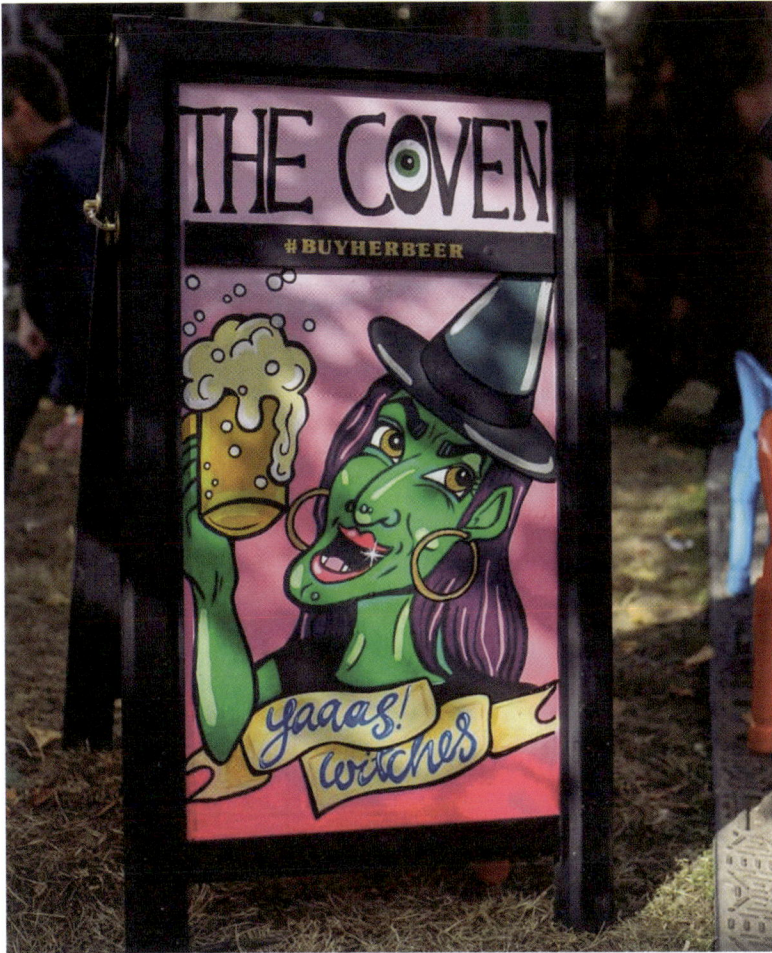

As The Coven started to generate new conversations about inclusion at festivals, the idea of Wellness Officers developed to try and address issues that brewery staff faced when customers got out of hand.

The Coven organises the training of Wellness Officers in first aid, mental health first aid and utilising adjusted elements of Active Bystanding techniques from the SafeBar Network, which is a non-profit based in the US. Wellness Officers are available to be hired to provide safety and wellness at beer-based events, and crucially deploy de-escalation skills to stop any issues developing – and then hopefully remove the need for attendees to be ejected from the venue. A problem best solved is a problem stalled from starting. We can provide risk assessments, look at problem areas within venues and be on duty through the event to attend to a wide range of issues. That might be providing a quiet area for those with sensory issues, or anyone who needs a break. We lend phone chargers, can give a bottle of water, be a taxi queue chaperone or execute crucial emergency first aid.

As The Coven is home to all, we naturally attract folk who are personally affected by our mission's goal. Our members; both Wellness Officers and Coven Ambassadors generally come from marginalised groups. Last count, 80% of members identified as a woman, 60% as non-binary or trans and 90% belonged to the LGBTQ+ community.

PIP YOUNG, 30SixCo

Diversity

The work of The Coven shows that helping women to feel welcome at beer festivals is not the only barrier that exists. Only 317 respondents who completed CAMRA's Inclusion, Diversity and Equality survey identified themselves as disabled. This equated to around 8% of the total respondents – well below the 20% or so of the UK population who describe themselves as disabled. But of them, nearly half said that their disability had had an effect on their ability to take part in CAMRA events.

Gary Keller works in the equality sector, and once led on Molson Coors' internal review on the subject. He has a hidden disability, but has not noticed many reasonable adjustments being made at festivals.

I attend local beer festivals as a disabled person. I can't think of any examples where they seem to have disability in mind, other than perhaps where wheelchair access has been thought about. But those that are in a chair often can't actually see to read what the beers are. Or if you're neurodiverse or dyslexic, you may not be able to read text on a white background.

Disability comes in many forms, but there are definitely tweaks that all beer festivals could make to make them more inclusive for all. Say having a pre-event for people that want to savour the atmosphere and enjoy the taste in quiet surroundings. Or having a braille guide.

GARY KELLER, drinks industry equality expert

CAMRA's review showed that access to seating is a big issue that puts off disabled people from attending beer festivals. The extended periods of time that volunteers are expected to stand while working behind a bar is putting off potential volunteers. It is reflective of the work society in general needs to do to be truly welcoming to all – without just providing step-free access and moving on.

The same applies to attracting a mix of people from different ethnic backgrounds to festivals. At the moment, CAMRA's review suggests that people visiting and volunteering at their festivals are much more likely to be from a white background than you would expect given the general demographics of the British population. This isn't a surprise to Anthony Adedipe, the co-founder of Eko Brewery.

If a festival is mainly targeted at a certain audience, then it's not surprising that that's the audience that they get. That's in the marketing and the way the festival itself is set up; what's on offer down to the detail of the food and the music. If people don't see themselves in something, then they're probably not going to feel as though it's a space for them.

It's hard to do if you haven't ever attracted a diverse audience. If you look at a photo or social media from a festival and it's all one demographic; if it's not the demographic you happen to be from, it might not be particularly appealing to attend that festival. But if there's a video that shows there's a mix of people at this festival and the offering itself is diverse, it might be a bit more appealing. People tend to want to go into spaces where they feel safe.

ANTHONY ADEDIPE, Eko Brewery

Nix Prabhu of Glasgow's Glasladies Beer Society certainly doesn't feel like she sees herself, an Indian woman, being targeted in marketing material for beer or for festivals.

I don't even think people of colour are targeted demographics. The closest thing we can come to is Bundobust, where the rich tradition of the South Indian subcontinent's cuisine is married to the beers. But even then that is very limited to the locations they have. I can count on one hand the people of colour in the beer industry in Scotland.

It's kind of funny, because people will say "Indian people don't drink" but India is superbly multicultural. So, of course there are some Indian people who do not drink for religious reasons. But trust me, there are an equal amount, if not more, who are very happy to imbibe. I mean one could argue that the entire state of Goa, where my mom's family is from, is pretty much run on Kingfisher beer.

NIX PRABHU, Glasladies Beer Society

So what is the answer? At the moment, we're pretty much at rock bottom in terms of ethnic diversity at festivals so there's a duty on all organisers to take an active approach to inclusivity.

'It's a reflection of society. There is nothing in the liquid being served at festivals that will make someone suddenly become aware of their surroundings and how they could make it more welcoming. The people going to the festivals go there with their friends. If they had friends from minority backgrounds, they would invite them along. The change we yearn for will come from proactively encouraging those not currently represented in these spaces to feel welcomed. Craft beer needs all the help it can get to ensure its survival.' (Stacey Ayeh, Rock Leopard Brewing Co.)

Glasladies Beer Society

Nix Prabhu sets an example for all to follow. She is leading the way in inclusive festivals. Nix is the founder of the Glasladies Beer Society, a community of women and non-binary people in Glasgow who came together in 2019 over a shared love of beer. The group organised the city's first women-run beer festival, Beer is for Everyone, in 2022. It was held at the Glasgow Beer Works Beer Garden and came about 'quite by accident,' Nix tells me. The group had wanted to do a local collaboration brew in 2021 to celebrate being able to meet up again

Nix Prabhu

after lockdown and to mark their second anniversary. Not one, but seven breweries came forward to work with them, and one of those suggested they run an event to showcase the collaborations.

We refrained from calling it a festival for many months, simply because we felt we were not qualified to run a festival. Maybe we put up invisible barriers for ourselves, underestimating just how capable we all are of putting on an event.

It wasn't until we talked about it, what we needed to do to actually make it happen, we thought this is very doable. Perhaps a lot of women feel they need permission to make a statement or plan an event. One of the biggest learnings that we had as a group was that if we waited around for anyone to give us permission we'd be waiting until kingdom come. And within five years, we've put on three festivals. It just shows what the power of groups like ours can be.

The first festival was sold out. It blew our minds that there were that many people in and around Glasgow who wanted to come to an event that we had organised. So we did another one and even before that had finished, folk were asking about the next one.

NIX PRABHU, Glasladies Beer Society

Beer is for Everyone has enjoyed steady growth, starting with 250, then 300 and finally up to 400 people. The 2024 edition of the festival took place at Drygate Brewing Co. It was the first time that they had breweries from England joining them and The Aeble Cider Bottle Shop of Anstruther, the first business of its kind in Scotland, put on the first cider bar. The Glasladies give their time, skills and expertise voluntarily because they want to keep on building their community. They want women and non-binary people to see themselves reflected in the traditionally male dominated beer space.

It took a long time to find a venue suitable for the event because accessibility is non-negotiable. In Glasgow, a lot of event spaces are found in older buildings and not necessarily modified for physical access.

Physical accessibility is just the first box on a long list of actions that the group takes to make sure that their festival is as inclusive as possible. They make the tap list available in large print and promote that. They haven't been able to print braille beer lists yet because the lead-in time is too long when some breweries can only finalise the beers they are bringing close to the event – that is an area that they are working on.

Music is kept at a lower level and strobe lighting is never used, to help guests who have hearing problems or sensory issues feel more comfortable. There is also a quiet room with no music, where people can take a few moments out. Beer is for Everyone is also dog friendly – not to mention having a public vote for the best dog on the day!

Having a consistent low- or no-alcohol option is another important facet of inclusivity. The Glasladies showcased their collaboration with Drygate at the first festival, an alcohol-free passion fruit and mango sour called Women Are Knackie. Scotland's only dedicated alcohol-free brewery, Jumpship, has also featured at two events. And of course, the food menu is inclusive too. While offering vegetarian, vegan and gluten free food is happily relatively standard these days, highlighting vegan and gluten free beers on the list isn't always prioritised. But of course the Glasladies have that under control too.

What else do we do? Well, you don't really think a beer festival and children go together, but our members tell us that finding childcare for over a couple of hours is not always possible. We want our members to be able to come to our festival so by holding them in family-friendly venues, that gives them the option of bringing their kids at least.

If childcare is needed a couple may make a decision that only one of them can go because one has to stay home to look after the kids. Anecdotally, we've heard that this is a situation that is disproportionately affecting women. If we're saying we're a women's group and we want to advocate for women in the beer space, we have to put our money where our mouth is.

NIX PRABHU, Glasladies Beer Society

The Glasladies' festival was also unique in putting out an invitation to women and non-binary people via a targeted social media post to let them know that they were welcome to attend by themselves.

We want to say: if you feel that you don't know anybody and that's why you're not coming to the festival, please come to the front desk, find us. We will introduce you to other group members who are at the festival and you will have readymade pals for the day.

We've heard it over and over again from folk who come to our meet-ups for the first time, they say they've been following us on social media for months but they're so nervous about going to things by themselves. So we are putting information out there to say to people, women especially, this would be the festival you come to by yourself, because we will look after you.

NIX PRABHU, Glasladies Beer Society

Learn and Discover

In 2018 CAMRA amended its key objectives. The organisational aim became 'to play a leading role in the provision of information, education and training to all those with an interest in beer, cider and perry of any type'. As such, a new officer was employed to run the Learning & Discovery project. Alex Metcalfe immediately embarked on piloting an informal learning programme at CAMRA festivals.

> It was very grassroots. We'd have face-to-face conversations with brewers and cider makers, access to fresh ingredients like season-al perry pears or hops and malt. We got lots of participation from leading and emerging brewing talent.
>
> Whether you've been drinking beer for 40 minutes or 40 years you can rock up to The Discovery Bar at a festival and do a comparative tasting, maybe comparing the same beer or cider across a couple of forms of dispense, or trying a barrel-aged version next to the non-barrel-aged, that sort of thing.
>
> ALEX METCALFE, Campaigns and Communications Manager: Learning & Discovery

The first festival pilot was in Manchester in January 2019. They held a comparative tasting on the festival floor. Despite just having a very modest stand to begin with, Alex describes it as 'pushing an open door'. Festival volunteers, the brewers and the visiting public loved the opportunity to interact with each other and to find out more. Another 15 festivals expressed an interest in having something similar at their event so they had to cap the number of pilots at seven to keep it manageable.

Despite this, with the support of the likes of Charles Faram, Murphy's and Son and Crisp Malt, they were able to showcase more than 30 varieties of hops, a range of malts and 45 breweries and cider makers in the first year. Work stopped during the pandemic as festivals were cancelled and Alex was redirected to produce online content for CAMRA members to access during COVID.

That online resource grew exponentially, while beer festivals were shakily getting back on their feet and learning to operate within

Brewers and volunteers on the Discovery Bar
in Belfast and Nottingham, 2024

the new landscape. Discovery Bars restarted and are now firmly rooted into CAMRA festival culture. Working collaboratively with festival organisers meant Discovery Bar Managers could run stands at festivals independently. A stock of equipment was purchased to support the activity, including branded bars, ingredients and display equipment. The evolution continues with the birth of the so-called CAMRA Village.

> We have a Discovery Bar space, the CAMRA shop, membership and information, all in one area to support each other. The theory being that having the bar in the midst of all that activity will help membership, recruitment and sales staff.
>
> Recently we did the Chelmsford Festival for the first time. It was the first time that I had been in one of those joint spaces. There was a lot of lovely camaraderie. They were letting everyone that signed up to CAMRA ring a bell, then everybody in the space would cheer.
>
> ALEX METCALFE, Campaigns and Communications Manager:
> Learning & Discovery

It's clear some breweries have really embraced the opportunity to get up close and personal with festival goers. Leigh-on-Sea Brewery have popped up at a number of festivals now, always turning up with a wide range of beers to taste, lots of branding to decorate the bar and merch for visitors to buy. The staff come from across the brewery team; technical and sales, bringing a depth of knowledge to the visitor and adding to this unprecedented opportunity for beer education.

HOW BEER FESTIVALS CHANGED OUR DRINKING HABITS

The Diversification of the British Beer Scene

When CAMRA's beer festivals first started, it was practically impossible for anyone to get beers from small breweries outside of their immediate distribution area. It took the positive action of dedicated volunteers driving up and down the nation, and sometimes taking trips to continental Europe, to fetch the casks themselves to supply their festivals and to bring new experiences to their attendees.

As well as demonstrating to brewers that there was a thirst for their products in other areas, CAMRA festivals helped to wake up the British palate to the quality and variety of beer that was available.

A little quote on mengodrinking.co.uk shows just what a revelation beer festivals were for drinkers in the 70s. Unfortunately, I've not been able to establish the identity of these four men from Aldershot, but their first experience led them to a lifetime of festivals and a conversion from keg lager to real ale.

> The first beer festival we went to was at The Farnham Maltings in 1977. As so often told, four of us were having our usual start to a Friday evening's drinking in the William Cobbett. Enquiring into the noise coming from across the road, we were told that a "beer festival" was on in The Maltings.

Never having heard of such a thing, the barman explained you could get to taste a lot of different beers, not just Courage Best. If we wanted to go, he still had some tickets left for the Friday session. Not wanting to miss our usual pub crawl we declined but did purchase some tickets for the Saturday lunchtime session.

As they say, the rest is history.   mengodrinking.co.uk

CAMRA's National Chairman in 1978, James Lynch, was one of those early pioneering volunteers who coaxed reticent small brewers into participating in festivals.

In September 1974 I persuaded a very reluctant Arkell's Brewery – still, as then, family owned and based on the outskirts of Swindon, with a local tied estate and next to no free trade way back then – to supply me with two firkins of their BBB beer for the beer exhibition being run by the then only three-month-old Newbury Branch of CAMRA at the Newbury Agricultural Show. They were very hesitant and said that Newbury was outside their trading area. It was, after all, 30 miles east of the brewery and their eastern and distant outpost at the time was a single handpump at The Bear Hotel in Hungerford, about 20 miles east of the brewery.

So sceptical were Arkells that on the day of the exhibition, the Free Trade Director, Deryck Arkell, Head Brewer, Don Kenchington, and the Second Brewer, Lou Mercer, and their respective wives turned up at the showground. I spotted them, showed them around the beer exhibition and gave them glasses of beer.

Such was the demand for real ale at the CAMRA exhibition that day, that the official caterers running the official beer tent for the entire show admitted defeat and closed up by 11am because there was no demand.

When I took the empty casks back on the Monday, I saw
Deryck Arkell, who'd spotted me unloading them from my
trusty Morris Minor Traveller, rushing down the outside stairs
from his office high up in the brewery building. He literally ran
over to me and vigorously shook my hand and profusely thanked
me for persuading him to supply beer. I asked for the invoice, with
my cheque book in hand and he waved it away and told me there
was no charge because we had done the brewery an immense
favour by giving it such unprecedented great publicity.

Arkells, within weeks, had totally revised their trading area
and approach to free trade and appointed Deryck's young son,
Nick – now the Free Trade Director – working alongside a new
appointment, Richard Turner, as their first ever free trade
manager. From that point on you could see Arkells drays
heading far and wide in all directions, including regular runs up
the M4 to London. They also started to extend their tied estate.
And this all happened as a direct result of the three-month-old
CAMRA Newbury Branch daring to hold a beer exhibition.

JAMES LYNCH, founder of the CAMRA Newbury Branch

That's not to say that this kind of seismic shift took place universally.
There was a slow evolution as consumer tastes diversified. Stoke's
Titanic Brewery still found it tough going to find their feet locally in
1985. Director Keith Bott described the impact that CAMRA festivals
had on their early success.

When we first started we were travelling to far-flung places to
sell our beer because the good people of Stoke at that time were
either Ansell's or Bass drinkers. And you weren't both, you were
one or the other. Getting them to try something new was nearly
impossible.

When we took over the brewery in 1988, I sold more beer into
Newcastle Upon Tyne than Newcastle Under Lyme. Consumers
genuinely weren't used to having a choice. There were the family
brewers, the Big Six, and a handful of the new small independents
like us. You used to go into the pub and you could have mild or
bitter. And if you didn't like those two you could mix them.

Festivals were a part of bringing choice to people before they realised that they wanted it. The success of beer festivals was born out of areas where choice wasn't so good. The CAMRA Stoke beer festival predated Titanic by a couple of years. We were rolling beer in in 36s in 1985, just because people were desperate for something a bit different.

I can remember brewing our first strong ale and our first mild. The Stoke festival was the launchpad for those beers. Publicans lived and breathed their own pubs back then, you wouldn't see a licensee outside of their own premises. So that opportunity to put beer in front of consumers was what mattered to us. You were relying on them to go back and tell the pubs.

KEITH BOTT, Titanic Brewery

In fact, parts of the licensed trade were so entrenched in the old ways that they nearly scuppered plans for the first Derby Beer Festival entirely, at first putting forward a strong opposition to the event.

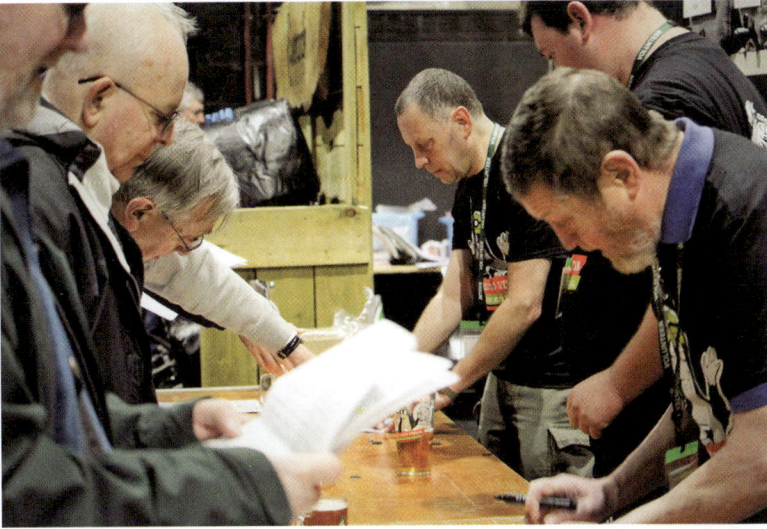

'The chair of the Derby Association of Licensed House Managers claimed, "A man (sic) is either a Bass drinker, a Shipstones drinker or an Ansells drinker … he is only going to go for one beer". They may have regretted these words, 22,000 pints from 39 breweries were drunk, and the licensees of the pubs around the venue were delighted with the roaring trade from the overspill.' (*Derby Drinker* 173, May/June 2017.)

Perhaps the editor of *The Scotsman*, Allan McLean, described this evolution best when he ruminated on his experience at the Caledonian Brewery Traditional Beer Festival in 1994. Scotland is still renowned for being, in places, a relative cask ale desert. But the situation has certainly improved since festivals came on the scene.

> Life is difficult for the dedicated beer enthusiast these days. Time was when it was all perfectly simple. The routine went like this: step into pub, order pint of 80/- ale, drink it and then order another of the same.
>
> These days, however, it's often a case of looking at the blackboard showing which guest ales are on tap and deciding whether to stick to something tried and trusted or something unheard of. Established breweries are constantly wheeling out new brews. New breweries are constantly wheeling out new brews. Established breweries previously limited to their own locality are wheeling out old brews in new areas.

This may sound like a complaint. Actually, it's a call for celebration. The variety of beers now available makes life far more interesting for the consumer. With these thoughts in mind, last weekend I stepped into the music-filled atmosphere of the Caledonian Brewery Traditional Beer Festival. The best yet of a series of very good events, incidentally. In the festival brochure I found a reference to Caledonian 80/-: "Described as 'Scotland's best pint'." I recognised the phrase – I wrote it: It was true at the time I penned it. Is it now?

Probably not. It isn't that there's anything gone wrong with this satisfying real ale. Nor is it even that the same brewery's previous Lorimer & Clark 80/- was something the memory buds on my tongue will forever recall with joy.

It's just that there are so many more beers now, that choosing the best must be a highly subjective decision. Anyway, some might say that Scotland's best pint these days is Deuchars IPA – from the same brewery.

ALLAN MCLEAN writing in *The Scotsman*,
Saturday, 11 June 1994

Creating a Network of Supply

As the demand for a more interesting range of beer grew, more new breweries stepped in to meet it. But it still wasn't practical for many of these nascent businesses to physically deliver their beer across a wide area.

It took three dedicated CAMRA members with a unique skill-set to solve the problem, and beer festivals were the catalyst. Tony Brookes, Tony Eastwood and Rob Walster were university friends who have been described as 'the godparents of beer wholesaling'. Their wholesale businesses – Legendary Yorkshire Heroes, Small Beer and the Prince of Wales in Stow Maries – were pivotal for breweries like Titanic, getting their beers out to the pubs and festivals across the country.

I was in CAMRA from the very early days. I was a transport economist by profession. We moved back to Newcastle in 1979 and it was an absolute real ale desert. You could count on the fingers of two hands the number of pubs in the whole Newcastle and Tyne area that had real ales at all. We realised there was a phenomenal market, so, in 1980 I changed roles completely and we set up what became a small chain of real ale off licences, the Legendary Yorkshire Heroes.

We changed the course of real ale. Part of our strategy was always driving around the country, bringing beers from independent groups and delivering it to beer festivals and other independent folks around the country. For example, at the Norwich Beer Festival in 1982 we supplied beers from Traquair House in Scotland, unbelievably rare.

We prised open some of the small and independent breweries from around the country who otherwise didn't supply beer to the wholesale trade, certainly not outside their areas. We were a safe pair of hands, we could look after their beers. It was all about making sure it arrived and was sold in good condition.

I used my transport economics knowledge to work with hauliers to import beers from Ireland. In one particular year the Great British Beer Festival put on a whole stand of Irish beers and we supplied virtually every one. The independent brewers there didn't actually produce their beer in cask form. They just let us rack off the beer from the settling tanks into our casks. We put the shives and keystones in and took the finings separate to put in when they were on the stillage at the festival. Talk about breaking down barriers, we were supplying beers that were unknown to most of the British beer drinking population.

TONY BROOKES, founder of Legendary Yorkshire Heroes,
later Head of Steam

It's hard to think of a single factor that did as much to encourage brewers to widen their nets, or to encourage the public to demand more choice, than the beer festivals of the late 70s and early 80s. This gave established brewers a bigger customer base and created assurance that new breweries would be viable. It was a key stepping stone to the beautifully diverse beer world that we are able to encounter at beer festivals and in our pubs today.

COUNTY DURHAM BRANCH

BARRY NEWMAN
CHAIRMAN

ANN FRANCIS
SECRETARY

The Campaign for Real Ale

37, BROOKSIDE
WITTON GILBERT
DURHAM
Durham 710509

Mr.T.Brookes,
Legendary Yorkshire Heroes Ltd.,
21 St. Georges Terrace,
Jesmond.

27th May 1982

Dear Tony,

7th Durham Beer Festival,
September 2nd-4th,
Dunelm House, New Elvet, Durham City.

I would like to place the following order for the above-mentioned event:

        3 Kilderkins Taylors Landlord
        1 Kilderkin Taylors Best Bitter
        2 Kilderkins Taylors Dark Mild
        2 Kilderkins Taylors Porter (or Ram Tam if Porter not available)
        2 Kilderkins Trough Wild Boar Bitter

to be delivered to Dunelm House on Tuesday 31st August. Because the festival has been extended this year to include a Thursday evening session, it is essential that the beers are delivered on Tuesday in order to allow to allow sufficient time for stillage.

I would be grateful if you could confirm as soon as possible that these arrangements are in order and let me know the current prices for the beers. Your invoice should be sent to Mr.C.Spedding, 2 Douglas Villas, Gilesgate, Durham City.

We would be very grateful if you could supply temporary bars and handpumps for the beers. In addition, you will of course, be very welcome to have your own stand and to supply any advertising material that you may wish to bring along. Finally, we are publishing a very comprehensive festival programme this year which will include advertising material and I understand that my wife, who is dealing with this programme, will be contacting you shortly to ascertain whether you wish to take space in this publication.

Best Wishes

Roger Francis
Festival Director.

The Legendary Yorkshire Heroes have been described as 'the godparents of beer wholesaling'

The Future

I think the beer festival scene is changing and the beer market is evolving. We're lucky because Fynefest is not just about beer, but about the whole experience with beer at its core. That builds an audience. If I ask you what's the favourite thing you've ever eaten, you're probably thinking of the setting that you were in, the people that you were with, the place that you were at. With FyneFest we're creating something where people think of that whole moment they enjoyed, and the beer is going to be the central part of that moment for them. I think beer festivals can go beyond just the bit of beer in a glass and offer something that helps people to tie the moment, the beer and the people together.

JAMIE DELAP, MD Fyne Ales

Beer and cider festivals are significant cultural events where the people of UK and Ireland have been creating deep memories for more than 50 years. The appetite for the choice of beers they offered was a key catalyst for the growth and proliferation of the independent brewing sector from the 1980s to (more or less) the present day.

Some events have achieved a legendary status. After 45 years, the Peterborough Beer Festival has become a major event in the city's annual calendar, for people from all walks of life. FyneFest routinely attracts more than 2,000 guests each year, many of them travelling several hundred miles to get to the Scottish glen where it is held. (I travelled about 325 miles each way, in case you were wondering.)

Many events are much smaller. More intimate. But they are no less important in connecting local communities and building bridges with local publicans and brewers.

Yet the future is not without its challenges. While we celebrated there being more than 2,000 UK breweries in 2016, at the time of writing we are back down to around 1,750. Many extremely popular independent and brewery-run festivals have become casualties of the current financial crisis. In 2024 Peakender, IndyManBeerCon, and even the Great British Beer Festival itself were unable to go ahead for one reason or another. The first two may not ever return.

Beer is inherently a social drink and in these pages we've seen the incredible network of relationships that festivals have helped to build. Festivals are a bit of fun, a frippery, an indulgence. But the 'nice-to-have' is always the first thing to go when times are hard, despite the obvious social value.

Volunteer-run festivals still have the edge when it comes to survival: the CAMRA festivals and grassroots events like the Independent Salford Beer Festival. Not having a wage bill to pay makes it much easier to balance the books, but still rising costs are impacting every area of event organisation. The price of beer, marquee hire, glassware. No beer festival is immune to these costs.

CAMRA has long known that its pool of volunteers is drawn from an ageing population. The hiatus in beer festivals enforced by COVID lockdowns was taken as a sign by many long-standing volunteers that it was time to hang up their mallets. Their numbers are depleted. Many popular beer festivals have struggled to stage a comeback since the pandemic. The Manchester CAMRA Beer and Cider Festival is a prime example. Once considered one of the greatest festivals in the country, there hasn't been a Manchester event since 2019. The organisers lost momentum during COVID and have struggled to find an appropriate, affordable venue and sufficient manpower ever since.

*   *   *

But it's not all bad news. In the 16 months I spent researching this book, I attended about 40 beer festivals across the UK and Ireland. There were hundreds more that I didn't visit. We've lost some great events in recent years, but there is still a thriving year-round offering to enjoy.

I've been to a lot of festivals, and I've worked at a fair few now too. In the final month before I finished writing this book, it dawned on me that I had become a part of the CAMRA festival family, almost by accident. I've been observing and writing about CAMRA for five years, yet somehow I was surprised how I've been welcomed into the organisation.

I thought I was an outsider. I took notes and photographs. I asked questions and peered into volunteer-only areas. But in reality I became an active participant in the planning, execution and enjoyment of some

Volunteer Sandra Cottam at GBBF (2023) on fancy dress Wednesday

of the festivals I have written about. The network of diverse friends I've made are my reward. We are unified by our love of beer and our burning desire to share that with the public. Beer festival culture is my culture.

The overwhelming majority of people I spoke to were positive about the future of beer and festivals. For those that run them, beer festivals are not optional extras. They are a passion. None of these enthusiastic, skilled and dedicated people will let our beer festivals go quietly into the night, despite the difficulties; they will go unashamed and raucous, probably singing off-key show tunes and swaying slightly as they always have. And they'll be back, ready for the next morning's session.

Appendices

Great British Beer Festivals

1975 Covent Garden, no GBBF (no specific organiser)
1977 Queen's Silver Jubilee Beer Festival (committee chaired by James Lynch)
1977 First GBBF Alexandra Palace, London (James Lynch)
1978 Alexandra Palace, London
1979 Alexandra Palace, London
1980 Alexandra Palace, London (Pat O'Neill)
1981 Queen's Hall, Leeds (Pat O'Neill)
1982 Queen's Hall, Leeds (Tim Webb)
1983 Bingley Hall, Birmingham (Tim Webb)
1984 NO EVENT
1985 Metropole, Brighton (John Cryne)
1986 Metropole, Brighton (John Cryne)
1987 Pitfield Metropole, Brighton (John Cryne)
1988 Queen's Hall, Leeds (Ted Eller)
1989 Queen's Hall, Leeds (Ted Eller & John Norman)
1990 Metropole, Brighton (John Norman)
1991 Docklands Arena [Now ExCeL], London (John Norman)
1992 Olympia, London (Christine Cryne)
1993 Olympia, London (Christine Cryne)
1994 Olympia, London (Christine Cryne)
1995 Olympia, London (Christine Cryne)
1996 Olympia, London (Paula Waters)
1997 Olympia, London (Paula Waters)
1998 Olympia, London (Paula Waters)
1999 Olympia, London (Alison Bridle)
2000 Olympia, London (Alison Bridle)
2001 Olympia, London (Alison Bridle)
2002 Olympia, London (Marc Holmes)
2003 Olympia, London (Marc Holmes)
2004 Olympia, London (Marc Holmes)
2005 Olympia, London (Marc Holmes)
2006 Earl's Court, London (Marc Holmes)
2007 Earl's Court, London (Marc Holmes)
2008 Earl's Court, London (Marc Holmes)
2009 Earl's Court, London (Marc Holmes)
2010 Earl's Court, London (Marc Holmes)
2011 Earl's Court, London (Marc Holmes)

2012 Olympia, London (Marc Holmes)
2013 Olympia, London (Ian Hill)
2014 Olympia, London (Ian Hill)
2015 Olympia, London (Ian Hill)
2016 Olympia, London (Ian Hill)
2017 Olympia, London (Ian Hill)
2018 Olympia, London (Catherine Tonry)
2019 Olympia, London (Catherine Tonry)
2020 NO EVENT
2021 NO EVENT
2022 Olympia, London (Catherine Tonry)
2023 Olympia, London (Catherine Tonry)
2024 NO EVENT (Catherine Tonry)
2025 NEC, Birmingham (Adam Gent)

National Winter Ales Festival/Great British Beer Festival Winter

1997–98 Old Fruit Market, Glasgow
1999–2002 Upper Campfield Market, Manchester
2003–04 Old Town Hall, Burton upon Trent
2005–09 New Century Hall, Manchester
2010–13 Sheridan Suite, Manchester
2014–16 The Roundhouse, Derby
2017–19 The Halls, Norwich
2020 New Bingley Hall, Birmingham
2021–22 NO EVENT
2023–24 Town Hall, Burton upon Trent
2025 Magna Science Adventure Centre, Rotherham

Christian Muteau Memorial Staff Award Winners

2002 Kevin Reeve (posthumous)
2003 Lynda Smith
2004 Fletch
2005 Roy Jenner
2006 John Cornish
2007 George Gendron
2008 Rob Whatley
2009 Paula Waters
2010 Mike Brady
2011 Denny Cornell
2012 Marc Holmes
2013 Mike Benyon
2014 Duncan Ward
2015 Dougie Smith
2016 Dave Sanders
2017 Malcolm Cron
2018 Nigel Croft
2019 Ruth Andrew
2022 Tony Hedger
2023 Barry Webb

About the Author

PHOTO BY LILY WAITE

Laura Hadland is a drinks writer and author who champions small producers and venues. She writes regular columns in *What's Brewing* and *Vineyard* magazine. Her first book, *50 Years of CAMRA*, was named the Best Beer Book in the World 2022 by Gourmand International and she was awarded CAMRA's prestigious Campaigner of the Year title in 2024.

Her work often examines the history of drinking culture and how it impacts our lives today. This is perhaps thanks to her former life as the Senior Curator for Leicester Arts and Museums Service where she gained an excellent grounding in archival research and oral history.

Laura writes about beer and pubs for a wide range of publications, including *The Telegraph*, *Pellicle* and *Ferment* magazine. She loves sharing the very best drinks with a great crowd at the tasting sessions she runs at pubs, festivals and events around the UK. In her spare time, Laura enjoys lino printing. Beer is a theme in her art as often as it is in her writing.

ACKNOWLEDGEMENTS

My heartfelt thanks go out to everyone who spoke to me, answered repeated follow-up questions, dug out old festival programmes, and generally humoured my nagging during the lengthy research for this book.

Index of People